A ROAD TO FREEDOM

A ROAD TO FREEDOM

Emotional, mental, spiritual, and physical restoration through the New Covenant

Merril van Rensburg

www.lifeskillcounsel.com

Copyright © 2023 by Merril van Rensburg

All rights reserved. No part of this publication may be reproduced, copied, and stored in any form or by any means, electronic, mechanical, photocopying or otherwise without prior permission of the author.

Email: *merril@lifeskillcounsel.com*

Front cover and artwork by Jenny Hawke

Creative Grace - http://www.creativegrace.co.uk/

First published in 2010
Revised in 2019, 2021, 2022

ISBN: 978-1-78324-279-5

Published by Wordzworth
www.wordzworth.com

This book is dedicated to all who persevere
to be that which the Father created them to be.

Contents

Foreword		3
Introduction		5
Part 1	**Emotional Restoration**	**9**
Chapter 1	The Paradox	11
Chapter 2	Foundational Principles for Restoration	15
Chapter 3	Spirit, Soul, and Body	19
Chapter 4	Environmental Effects	23
Chapter 5	Life Script, Subconscious, and the Heart	26
Chapter 6	Conception and Life in the Womb	30
Chapter 7	Physical Needs, Fear, Guilt and Shame	36
Chapter 8	Spiritual Roots and Influences	41
Chapter 9	A Place to Start	47
Chapter 10	Emotional Restoration	52
Chapter 11	Renewing the Mind - Repentance	63
Part 2	**Spiritual Restoration**	**69**
Chapter 12	Understanding the Spiritual Kingdoms	70
Chapter 13	Tactics, Soul Ties & Strongholds	75

Chapter 14	The Human Spirit	84
Chapter 15	The Dysfunctional Spirit	90
Chapter 16	Spiritual Restoration	95

Part 3	**Physical Restoration**	**103**
Chapter 17	Healing Body Memories	104
Chapter 18	God's View on Physical Healing	109
Chapter 19	Why Are Only Some Healed?	112
Chapter 20	Restoration and Self Care	118

Part 4	**Appendices**	**125**
Appendix 1	Case Study	126
Appendix 2	Sample Prayers	129
Appendix 3	Unpleasant Feeling Words	149
Appendix 4	Abridged List of Spiritual Strongholds	151

Foreword

"A Road to Freedom" was first outlined in 1998. It was revised 2008 as my knowledge and understanding of grace grew. In 2021, I have gained even more understanding regarding how you function spiritually, in your soul and physically, particularly how your brain and bodies store information that impacts how you live life. This information I have applied my own life which has helped me mature and live life abundantly. In the following pages, it is hoped that my personal experiences and knowledge of the New Covenant will help you to live the life you always knew was there for you. My intention is that this book will help you unravel some of the mysteries behind your life struggles, and find some simple steps to achieve emotional, mental, spiritual, and physical healing. As you begin your journey, keep in mind that each one of us is uniquely different, and that you have different experiences and skills. The degree of success in overcoming your difficulties will largely depend upon your ability to apply the principles in this book.

If you find that you are not experiencing the desired restoration, I urge you to seek outside help. We have been created to live in supportive relationships and not in isolation. Asking for help can be difficult when you have been hurt, but sometimes your struggles can only be resolved in safe and trusting relationships. It may be frightening, time consuming and risky but it is necessary. My advice is to begin slowly, take small steps and ask the Lord to bring the right people into your life so that you can learn to trust again.

I wish you every success as you step out on your personal Road to Freedom!

Living to please the Father's heart,

Merril

Introduction

GOD'S PLAN OF REDEMPTION

I am excited that you have decided to journey through this book with me. Maybe, this is your first exploration of God and Christianity, and you are wanting to find out all that it has for you. If this is your first experience, then this introduction was written especially for you.

Christianity is different from all other religions. Religion dictates that there is a ruling god or gods that needs to be obeyed to be acceptable and if acceptable you escape punishment. Christianity says that you cannot ever be good enough because of brokenness and sin. Christianity offers an alternative to trying to avoid punishment by being good.

Think about it this way. If you are arrested for a crime and found guilty, you will be punished. Just because you paid your taxes or helped an old person across the road, that will not nullify the crime nor avoid the punishment. We are punished for what we do wrong and not excused if do something good. Well, that leaves you in a no-win situation, unless …?

Christianity, Judaism, and Islam are all monotheistic. Christianity accepts that God is 3 parts, God the Father[1], God the Son[2] and God the Holy Spirit[3]. This is referred to as a Triune God.

Here is a way that this can be understood. Water has a chemical composition of H^2O. Water can take the form of ice, liquid or steam but remains H^2O. Each can exhibit different properties and be used for

---

[1] 1 Corinthians 8:6
[2] John 10:30
[3] 2 Corinthian 13:14

different purposes, but still in its essence, is the same. Just like you; you are spirit, soul, and a physical body. You are three parts. Each part has different functions, but you are still one person.

In a time before time, God began to create the heavens, the world and all that is. God also created animals, birds, bugs, and creepy crawly things. But God also wanted something that was not governed by instinct. God wanted something that was independent, something with a free will, that could freely choose Him, or something that could choose otherwise. So, God created you! And He created you with a free will.

Now, God is all knowing, ever present, and all powerful[4]. He could foresee that mankind would want to follow personal desires and ambitions. These choices would eventually result in causing harm and hurt to self and others, which we call sin. This sin results in a separation from God because God is perfect and unselfish, and sin is imperfect. Perfection and imperfection cannot abide together and as a result the relationship God wanted with you, could not happen.

We all know that wrong must be punished. But how about this; let us say you had a very big speeding fine and someone else pays that fine in full. Would the court be able to send you to prison? Because the law is fulfilled, there cannot be any further punishment. But there is a proviso: the person who pays the fine must be innocent, otherwise they will be "paying" for his own crimes. Obviously, the bigger the crime, the bigger the punishment. The ultimate punishment is death.

So, God came up with a cunning plan which was hatched before the foundation of the world. God decided that He would send a part of Himself, God the Son, to earth, to live just like you, facing the same temptations as you, but He had to be sinless. And He had to do this with no "superpowers". He had to be just like you!

---

[4] Psalm 139 God's Omniscience, Omnipresence and Omnipotence

INTRODUCTION

So, Jesus, God the Son, came to earth as a mortal person, leaving all His deity behind. He was born in a natural manner except that the fertilization of the ovum was supernatural and not by a human sperm. This is important because if the ovum was fertilised by human sperm, He would be carrying the corrupted DNA of the male line of a broken human, and then he would have died for His own human brokenness, not yours. Here on earth, he had to face everything that you have had to face. The physical events may be different to yours, but He had to face all the emotional turmoil, rejection, insults that every person has had to face. He also had to face the challenge and not retaliate in His own defence. On top of all that he had to face the severest torture imaginable, to the point of death.

Now we know that everything is governed by scientific laws. Also, that society is governed by moral and ethical laws. Without these laws there would be chaos. Similarly, there are spiritual laws. One of these laws dictates that transgression of these laws must be punished by death. So, Jesus died but He had not transgressed any law, so He was innocent! Obviously, the reverse is also true. If you have not broken any law, you cannot be punished. As result we have this anomaly. Jesus can now turn round and say, "I have paid the full penalty of death for someone who deserves to be punished."

There is one final piece to this amazing redemption plan. It is that you have the free will to accept or reject this offer of salvation[5]. It is all up to you. Your own free choice.

There is an added bonus. If you accept this offer, God is able to redeem all that is broken in your life. And that is what the rest of this book is about!

---

[5] There is a prayer in Appendix 2, that you can pray so that you can be part of God's Plan of Redemption

A ROAD TO FREEDOM

*A fire insurance policy:
Jesus Christ Mutual Life
The premiums are all paid up
and the benefits are out of this world!*

— Author unknown —

Part 1

EMOTIONAL RESTORATION

Chapter 1

THE PARADOX

To many people, life seems and often is unfair. Many things happen to you that are undeserved. Life can suck, but the good news is that you don't have to be sucked in.

These events, hurts, traumas, and disappointments impact your thinking which in turn impacts our lives. Negative thinking manifests as fears, anxieties, depressions, various mental health problems, inappropriate behaviours, and relationship difficulties. Mostly we are unaware what the initial cause is and usually blame current circumstances.

Research has shown that over 75% of our mental health and behavioural difficulties results from our negative thinking patterns[6]. Negative thinking also impacts your DNA. With negative thought patterns DNA codes can be switched on and off, resulting in poor quality of wellbeing, which is reflected in physical health. This can also be passed on genetically[7].

None of you choose to suffer, but suffer you do. What I have set out is a path you can follow so that you may be free from the effects of the

---

[6] "Switch on your Brain" Dr Caroline Leaf, 2015
[7] https://www.powerofpositivity.com/heres-how-your-thoughts-affect-your-dna/

past that impact the present. Come with me and let us explore this journey together. I have been there, and I know the freedom it offers.

Many people come to me for counselling to solve their problems. They ask, "Can you help me?" My reply is always, "No, but I do know the One who can! My purpose is not to solve your problem for you. My purpose is to show you how you can go to God who can solve your problem and all your other problems as well."

I often describe my task in the following way: "Do you see that light?" I ask, as I point to the ceiling. "That light is connected by wires to a power station. The light is the solution to your problem. The power station is your Heavenly Father. The light switch is your will. No one ever takes much notice of the wires. I am that wire and can be replaced at any time. The important elements are the light, (your solution) and the source (your Heavenly Father)."

I was told I can lay hands on the sick and they will recover[8]. I became dissatisfied when they did not. I knew the Scripture was true but felt that something was missing. As I searched, the Holy Spirit began to reveal to me many truths. The Holy Spirit led me to the work of many others who have gone before, and I owe much to the inspiration and wisdom that I have gained from them. What I am sharing here is a compilation of many things I have found that can yield the desired results when correctly applied.

I am not satisfied with dealing with symptoms. I am always looking for the root, or the cause, of the problem. I have found that when the root is dealt with, recovery follows naturally. The Holy Spirit has taught me how to find the root cause of the problem through looking at the symptoms[9], and then to apply Biblical principles to bring about restoration.

A practical example:

If you have a tree that produces bad fruit (symptoms), you can pluck off the bad fruit (deal with the symptoms). But the problem is that next year, it produces the

---

[8] James 5:14-15
[9] Matthew 7:16-17

THE PARADOX

same bad fruit again. You can try to cut off the branches but soon the tree will produce new branches and eventually more bad fruit. Cutting the tree down but leaving the stump is also not the solution as the tree can begin to grow again. But if you dig out the roots, then the whole tree dies, and the bad fruit disappears.

First, we will look at how you function and then at how you are able to change what you are struggling with.

The first precept you need to remember is that you are spirit, soul, and body[10]. Although working with one aspect of your being does impact the other two, other work will need to be applied in the other areas. For example, the body has somatic (body) memories[11] that will need specific techniques to be released and thus bring healing.

The next precept that you need to hold, is that the Holy Spirit will direct you to various actions that are different from just asking for healing. For example, you may be directed by the Holy Spirit to speak to someone, seeking restitution, or take some rest.

I have drawn several diagrams to help you understand what makes you tick. Freely I have received and freely I give[12].

As you read these pages, my hope is that you will grow in understanding of your Heavenly Father's mercy and grace. My prayer for you is that you may become more intimately acquainted with Him. My desire is to see people set free from the troubles that burden them. My passion is to do His will.

Our opinions become fixed at the point we stop thinking!

— Ernest Renan —

---

[10] 1 Thessalonians 5:23
[11] The Body Keeps the Score – Bessel van der Kolk, 2015
[12] Matthew 10:8

A ROAD TO FREEDOM

A time to consider

Where have you been searching to find answers to your problem?

_____
_____
_____
_____

Who have you been depending upon to find a solution?

_____
_____
_____
_____

How effective has your search been so far?

_____
_____
_____
_____

Chapter 2

FOUNDATIONAL PRINCIPLES FOR RESTORATION

We, as believers, may often struggle to come to terms with what we read in the Bible and the reality of what is taking place in your lives. When you are sick, you run to the doctor, but the Bible says that you are healed by what Jesus did for you[13]. Although the Bible tells you not to worry[14], you worry and are fearful. The more you try to fulfill what the Bible teaches, the more it appears you fail. Often, you compensate by either wearing a mask or by withdrawing and feeling a failure. Alternatively, you may begin to doubt the truth of the Bible or even adopt some alternative doctrine to explain your situation.

I believe your struggle can be summed up in the words of Isaiah when he says you are trapped because you do not understand[15]. Hosea says you are destroyed because you have no comprehension of the situation[16].

---

[13] 1Peter 2:24
[14] Matthew 6:25
[15] Isaiah 5:13
[16] Hosea 4:6

A ROAD TO FREEDOM

A practical example:

If you have a motorcar and it breaks down, how will you be able to fix it if you have no idea how it works? But if you understand the principals involved then given the correct tools, you may be able to tackle the breakdown. Alternatively, you will know enough to be able to seek the correct help.

The purpose of this book is that you may understand how you have been created and how you function so that you may learn how to solve your problems and begin to live out the abundant life that Jesus has given you[17].

Before you can obtain resolution or get healing from your emotional problems, there are some foundational principles that might be helpful for your understanding:

1. When you were created, you were given free will. No living person can violate your free will. Even your Heavenly Father has chosen not to override that will. He did not create you to be some super-functioning robot that would instinctively worship Him. He wanted you to be able to make decisions freely, and to be free to choose Him. This is a unique privilege.

2. Irrespective of what you are experiencing or seeing, you need to choose to believe that what the Bible says is the absolute truth[18]. As a word of caution, please be careful not interpret scripture to your own subjective understanding.

3. Because you have free will, you can hold on to the truth that there is restoration, that there is a solution, that there is a way out from your pain or problem.

---

[17] John 10:10
[18] Due care should be exercised in Biblical interpretation. A correct exegesis and hermeneutical study may often be required to fully understand Scripture – author's comment.

4 We will need to take responsibility for your own emotions. I often ask the question: *"If you spit on me, what will you make me?"* I usually get very puzzled looks and eventually a response like 'disgusted' or 'angry'. My answer is, *"No, all your spit will do is make me wet. The disgust or anger is my own emotional response to your spit"*. We are very good at shifting blame, "He made me angry." "It's his fault." "It's God's fault." "The devil made me do it." Until you take responsibility for your own emotions, your Heavenly Father is unable to help you. By taking responsibility you are at the point of inviting God to change you.

5 Unless Jesus comes and changes you, you are always going to remain the same. You cannot change yourself deep inside. You may be able to modify your behaviour, develop new coping skills and put on facades, but inside you will still be the same.

Learn from the mistakes of others.
We can't live long enough to make them all yourselves.

— Martin Vanbee —

A ROAD TO FREEDOM

A time to reflect

What are your thoughts on healing and emotional restoration?

_____

_____

_____

What unique attribute do we as humans have that no other creature has?

_____

_____

_____

How would you feel or respond if someone spat on you?

_____

_____

_____

How do you think Jesus reacted when they spat on him in Matthew 27:30?

_____

_____

_____

Chapter 3

SPIRIT, SOUL, AND BODY

We are created spirit, soul, and body[19]. Your spirit is that part of you that causes you to feel alive. Your soul, which is your personality, has three areas of functioning, your mind, your will, and emotions. The spirit and soul cannot be seen with the human eye. Your body, emotions and behaviour are the windows to the condition of your spirit and soul. The spirit, soul and body are linked. If you touch one part, the other parts are also affected. There is a diagram at the end of the chapter to help illustrate this concept.

A practical example:

If I take a pin and jab it into your arm, the first thing you will feel is pain. Immediately, there will be an emotional response of either fear or anger. Your mind analyses the situation and you spontaneously make a willful decision to either run away or hit me. Your spirit could also be wounded since it was unexpected of me, whom you trusted. Through this physical pain, your soul and spirit are touched, and you react physically.

Let us now look at this connection of spirit, soul, and body from a different

---

[19] 1 Thessalonians 5:23

angle. When you are sick, you will go to the doctor who gives you some form of medication to cure the illness. As the body recovers, you begin to feel happier and are able to think more clearly. The result of clear thinking is better decision making. The final consequence is that your spirit functions better. Your spirit has nine different functions, and these are discussed in more detail in Chapter 14. Various drugs can also be used to alter your mental and emotional state, which can cause you to feel physically better.

Medical science recognizes that the problem may not only be physiological, and you may be referred for some sort of therapy. The applied psychological interventions can help alter the way you think, feel, and react. Using cognitive therapy, the therapist will be helping you to manage your thoughts and think positively. Cognitive therapy works with the processing of sensory information, perception awareness and judgment. If you can process information more accurately, you will then be able to make better decisions. Making better decisions could result in greater emotional stability, a healthier body, and a more buoyant spirit. Cognitive therapy is using the Biblical principal of learning to think differently[20].

Emotive therapy, which works with the emotions, is intended to help you focus on positive feelings about events and situations. Being emotionally stable could result in improved thinking, better decision-making, improved physical health and a flourishing spirit. Emotive therapy has is using the Biblical principal that the joy of the Lord is your strength[21].

Behaviour therapy can help you improve the way you live through reinforcement, helping you to make better choices and decisions. The essence of the Bible is to guide you in making good and correct choices so that you do not suffer unpleasant consequences[22]. By making healthy choices, you feel emotionally secure, resulting in clearer thinking, being physically healthier and causing your spirit to prosper.

---

[20] Romans 12:2, Philippians 4:8
[21] Nehemiah 8:10, Colossians 1:11
[22] Deuteronomy 28

SPIRIT, SOUL, AND BODY

We can feed our spirits through singing praise and worship songs, meditating of God's Word, praying and being in a Godly environment. Feeding your spirits in this way will cause your spirit to be enriched, which generally results in your soul and body becoming healthier.

The diagram below illustrates the interaction between spirit, soul, and body. The spirit and the soul are non-spatial and for ease of understanding are illustrated diagrammatically as separate circles. Most probably this is not totally correct as they may integrate with the body in a complex manner.

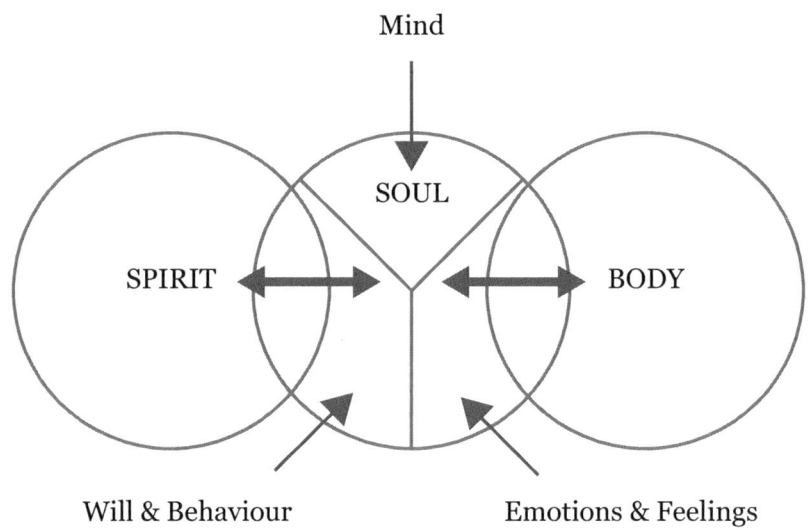

Great minds discuss ideas. Average minds discuss events.
Small minds discuss people.

— Eleanor Roosevelt —

A ROAD TO FREEDOM

A time to Ponder

Write down the events of a time when thinking became distorted due to an unpleasant experience.

_____
_____
_____
_____

Write down the events of a time, that you can remember, when you behaved in a way you wish you had not.

_____
_____
_____
_____

Write down the events of a time when your feelings became disturbed due to an unpleasant experience.

_____
_____
_____
_____

Chapter 4

ENVIRONMENTAL EFFECTS

The environment in which you live influences you. This environment consists of several sub-systems that impact your thinking, your behaviour and how you feel daily. These sub-systems are continually changing so that how you feel or react to a situation on a Sunday may be completely different to Monday.

Let us examine some of these sub-systems. The town or city in which you live will have a direct influence on your behaviour. In a city with a high crime rate, you will be more alert, suspicious, and cautious, while in a town where there is less crime, you will generally be more relaxed. Your friends and family will influence you, positively if they are supportive, and negatively if the relationship is destructive. Similarly, your working conditions can cause you to feel frustrated, unfulfilled, or positive. If you are in an encouraging church environment, you can face the ups and downs of life more confidently. Your social status will also shape the way you think and behave.

Your cultural background and perceptions of life play an important part in your ability to cope. A culture is an accepted set of norms within a group that helps the group to function harmoniously. There are many different cultures, and no culture is more significant than any other.

The diagram below illustrates how your culture and environment can impact your souls.

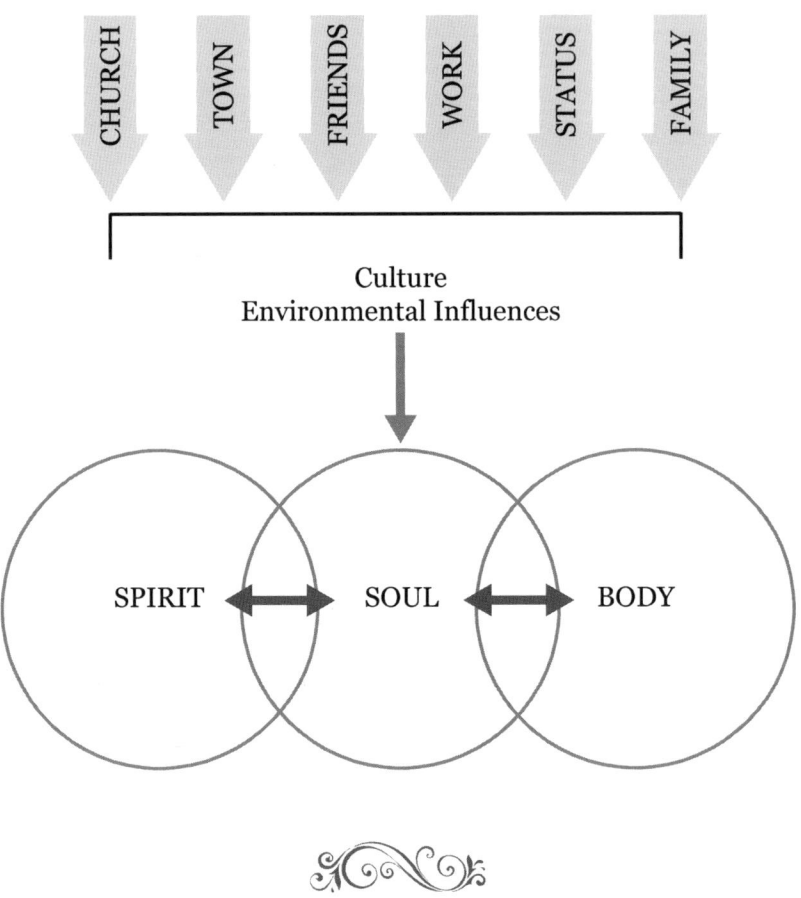

We cannot fear the future if we know what happens at the end.

— Author unknown —

ENVIRONMENTAL EFFECTS

A time to reflect

Write down an area of influence your friends and family have upon you.
_____
_____

Write down the extent to which the town or suburb where you are living affects your behaviour.
_____
_____

Write down 3 of the pressures that your culture has placed upon your everyday life.
_____
_____

To what degree do you believe your social status dictates the decisions that you make?
_____
_____

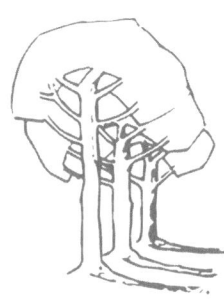

Chapter 5

LIFE SCRIPT, SUBCONSCIOUS, AND THE HEART

Have you ever noticed yourself repeating a habit that you have promised yourself not to do again? Or maybe you said to yourself, "I would never do that", only to find yourself doing it? In the Bible you have the story of Peter saying to Jesus that he would not desert him[23], only to find that a couple of hours later he did just that! Have you ever wondered why this happened?

Up to now, I have only talked about how you are affected by the present. You have all lived many years and so you have a historical past. It is interesting that approximately 90% of your present decisions and actions are based on your past experiences[24]. Only 10% of your present decisions and course of actions are influenced by current circumstances. What is even more disconcerting is that your spontaneous reactions will override all known facts and information[25]. What is in the heart dominates what

---

[23] Matthew 26:33-35, 69-75
[24] Transactional Analysis explains how your adult patterns originate in childhood – 'A New Introduction to Transactional Analysis' by Stewart, Jones
[25] Transactional Analysis is based on the understanding of a 'Life Script' and that we continue to repeat childhood strategies, even when they result in pain or defeat – ibid

LIFE SCRIPT, SUBCONSCIOUS, AND THE HEART

you know with your mind. You can memorize Scripture, but that seldom changes your automatic responses when distressed or caught off guard.

Here is an illustration:

A group of children from a disadvantaged community are seated in a circle on the floor of a room. You then tell them that you are going to give them sweets. You tell them that the sweets are all the same and that there are so many that they will not be able to eat them all or carry them away. You then tell them that there is no need to grab as there is more than enough sweets for everyone. Having made sure that they understand, you drop the sweets on the floor in the middle of the circle. What do they do? The children's past experiences of lack and the need to fight for survival, spontaneously kicks in and they grab the sweets.

This story shows how the past has a direct influence upon you. I will now explain how this happens.

Our past, or life-script, is a record of events, experiences, decisions, thoughts and adopted customs. This life-script may be subconscious, in other words, you may not be consciously aware of what is recorded there. The Bible refers to this as "our heart"[26]. Scripture tells you that your heart has been corrupted[27] and what you say is governed by your life-script[28]. You could think of your life-script as being like the hard-drive of a computer. On the hard-drive various programs are recorded. You may be busy working on one program and if a virus enters the computer, the virus program stored on the hard drive will automatically spring into action, disrupting your work. Similarly, when a certain event occurs, a past memory associated with that event springs up and you react out of your learnt response. You may have an experience of being attacked by a person with a pin. Years later, if you are accidentally pricked, you react out of that experience and coping mechanisms that you will have developed to deal with such an

---

[26] There are over 760 different scriptures about the heart in the Bible
[27] Jeremiah 17:9
[28] Matthew 12:34, Luke 6:45

event. Your life-script is a record of normative (normal) and idiosyncratic (peculiar) events that may be either pleasant or unpleasant, and which will affect how you may respond in any current experience.

The diagram below illustrates how past events are written on your life-script and how they impact the present.

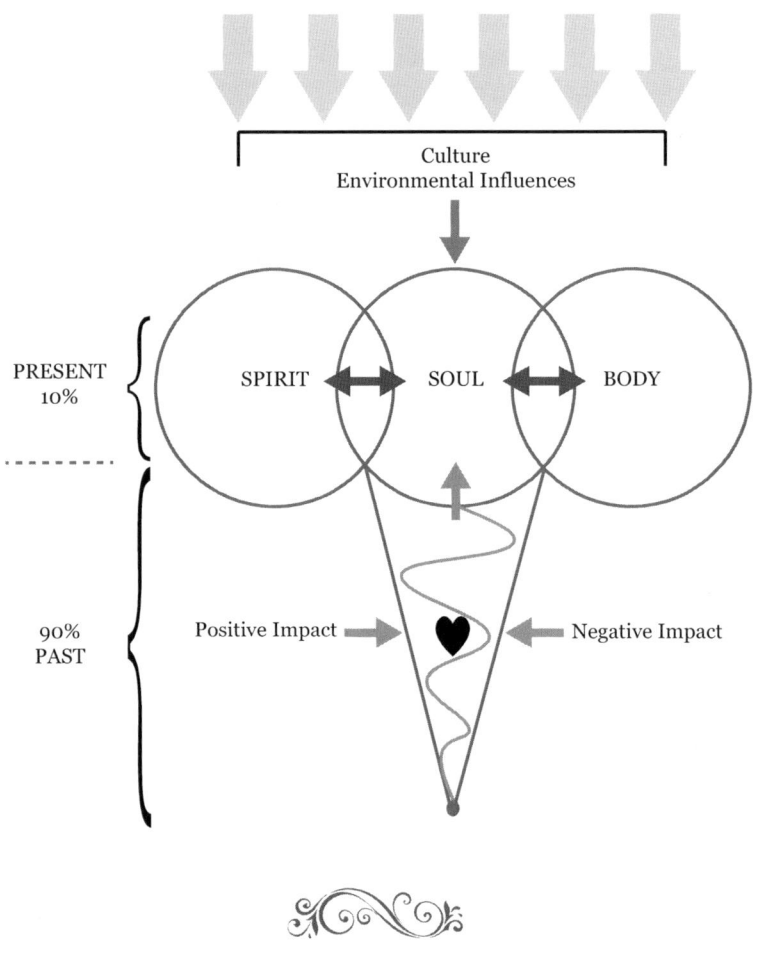

*Don't question what you know
in the light when you find yourself in darkness.*

— Author unknown —

LIFE SCRIPT, SUBCONSCIOUS, AND THE HEART

A time to meditate

Write down the habits that you have tried to get rid of that keep re-occurring.

_____
_____

Record the time you first became aware of your most annoying habit.

_____
_____

Write down what you think may be a particular event that caused that habit.

_____
_____

Record other events from your past that may be causing you stress.

_____
_____

Chapter 6

CONCEPTION AND LIFE IN THE WOMB

In the last chapter we looked at the effect of your past on the present and it was noted, that whether you realise it or not, it still has a dynamic effect. The question is when did your past begin to make an impact, or alternatively, when did my life on earth begin? You may think that your life started on the day you were born, but this is not true. Your life started a short time after conception.

At conception the father's sperm fertilises the mother's ovum, usually in the fallopian tubes. As fertilisation takes place, the DNA of the mother and the father intermingle, and this determines the genetic structure of the child. If two X-chromosomes are present the child is a girl and if an X-chromosome and a Y-chromosome is present, the child is a boy. The DNA determines the bone structure, the colour of the eyes, hair, skin, etc. This fertilised egg is now called an embryo and begins to subdivide, multiplying itself into many cells. The embryo continues to move on its way down the fallopian tube until it enters the womb, where it will attach itself to the womb lining. If it cannot attach itself to the womb, it will be discharged from the body in the normal process.

CONCEPTION AND LIFE IN THE WOMB

When it attaches itself to the womb, then life as a human being can begin. It is at this point, I believe, that the Heavenly Father looks in and chooses you – soul and spirit. He can see the circumstances of the conception; whether it was wanted or an unwanted pregnancy and the surrounding events. He knows the possible decisions the mother could make, and whether the father is present and supportive. God also sees the financial situation, the circumstances the child will grow up in, even the political climate of the country.

God chooses and equips you with a personality that can cope with the life circumstances you are born into. Scripture tells us that there is no temptation that you cannot overcome[29]. God, the Father, has plans for you to be successful and not to be harmed[30]. Personally, I believe that no one is an accident and that the Father has created each one of us with a plan and a purpose, irrespective of the reasons behind the conception.

Scripture clearly shows you that God gives you your spirit[31] and your soul[32]. Verse 15 of Psalm 139 says, "my frame was not hidden" from the Father. The word 'frame' in Hebrew means your mind and intellectual construction. The word is a derivative from another Hebrew word meaning 'squeezing into shape that which was pre-ordained.' If you look further into verse 16 of the same Psalm, it says that He saw your unformed substance. The suggestion here is that God knows your DNA, your physical attributes and everything else about you.

When the embryo attaches itself in the womb, it then becomes a foetus. What you need to remember is that your spirit and soul today, is the same spirit and soul present at your conception. Your spirit and soul do not grow like your body. Your foetus is hardwired with emotions for life enhancement and survival. You can think, make subconscious decisions,

---

[29] 1 Corinthians 10:13
[30] Jeremiah 29:11
[31] Ecclesiastes 12:7, Zechariah 12:1
[32] Psalm 139:13-16

and feel pain. Your spirit and soul need to learn how to live in a human body and this process will take you many years. The development of the foetus is amazingly fast. At 6 weeks after conception, blood is being produced and your heart is beating. At 8 weeks after conception, your brain is thinking, and these brain waves have been scientifically recorded. By the 10th week after conception, you are about 2 centimeters long and your internal organs, fingers and toes have been formed. By the 12th week you can stretch, kick and leap around in your mother's womb, although your mum is still unaware of any movement[33]. There are ultrasound images of unborn babies appearing to suck, scratch, smile, and cry at 26 weeks[34]. You are a complete human being. All you cannot do is live outside the environment of your mother's womb.

You probably know about what is commonly referred to as a sixth sense. This receiving of information or being aware of something without smelling, hearing, seeing, tasting, or touching is one of the functions of your spirit[35]. It is important to bear in mind that your spirit, when you were a baby, had not yet been hampered by the brokenness of this world and was fully functioning. From my work in dealing with trauma that has occurred while in the womb, there is evidence to suggest that the baby is able to pick up what the mother is experiencing and processes this information[36].

Another aspect that needs to be understood is that the patterns of your thinking, your experiences, traumas and decisions impact your genes, and this is then passed onto your future generations[37], which in turn impacts the lifestyle choices of your children. In science, this is known as epigenetics[38].

---

[33] BBC News Channel - Scans uncover secrets of the womb
[34] ibid
[35] I Corinthians 2:11
[36] "Mothers can pass along their experiences to their children …" research report in The Journal of Neuroscience.
[37] Exodus 34:7
[38] https://nobaproject.com/modules/epigenetics-in-psychology

CONCEPTION AND LIFE IN THE WOMB

Here is an illustration:

Let us think about a teenager or woman, who has had sexual intercourse and does not want to be pregnant. She misses her monthly period but thinks little of it. It could be some 8 weeks before she begins to think that she may be pregnant. As she considers she may be pregnant, anxiety, tension and fear begin to well up within her. She takes a pregnancy test and it comes back positive. Several thoughts will be tumbling through her mind and possibly, "I don't want this thing". The baby in her womb could pick up on these emotions and develop feelings of "I am not wanted; I am a mistake". This child's spirit and soul has come from heaven with a spiritual understanding of the Father's plans and purposes for their life. This leaves confusion and feelings of rejection within the baby which impacts their life. When you experience rejection, you will often adopt rebellious and aggressive attitudes or cultivate a lack of self-worth. From this point on, your life becomes increasingly difficult. Possibly you will create unhelpful coping mechanisms. These coping mechanisms are like walls that you build around you. They can keep you from being hurt but they also trap you inside. Unfortunately, these walls also tend to keep God out.

There is ongoing research that suggests that the baby in the womb knows if it is a wanted child and if the father is at hand. It is also suggested that the baby is aware which sex the parents would prefer[39]. A child instinctively wants to please its parents. Failure to meet parents' expectations could result in destructive, performance-orientated behaviour.

What should be understood is that every child is initially created in the heart of a loving Heavenly Father. The child knows instinctively that it should have two parents who should give unconditional love. The child knows it should be nurtured, protected, understood, and encouraged. When these God-created expectations are not met, it may result in negative feelings, which could result in judgmental attitudes. The child, in later life, might subconsciously try to convey its disapproval of the parents' behaviour through tantrums or outbursts of anger. The usual result is a reprimand,

---

[39] "Remembering Your Life Before Birth: How Your Womb Memories Have Shaped Your Life and How to Heal Them" - Michael Gabriel, 1995

which may further exacerbate the situation. Alternatively, the child may internalize all their frustrations, which can be equally destructive causing a disruption to the endocrine system, which could lead to physical illnesses[40].

The diagram below shows conception and birth in relation to your life-script.

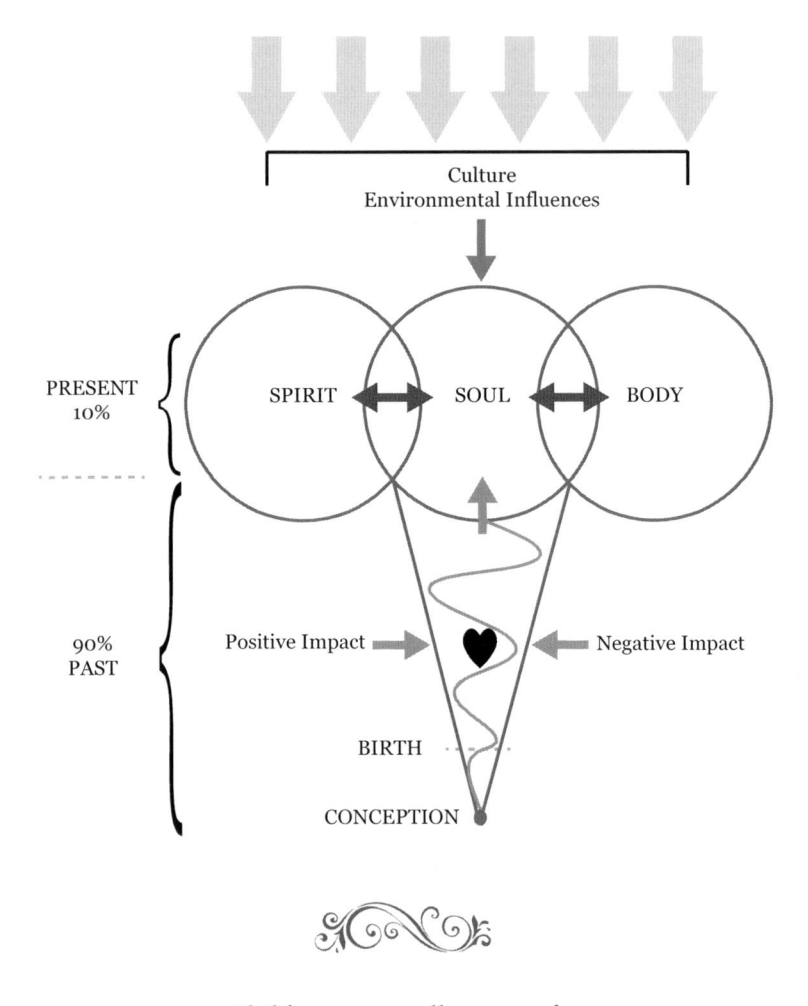

```
                    ↓ ↓ ↓ ↓ ↓ ↓ ↓
                          Culture
                   Environmental Influences
                            ↓

PRESENT          SPIRIT ↔ SOUL ↔ BODY
  10%

              Positive Impact →  ♥  ← Negative Impact
  90%
  PAST
                          BIRTH
                       CONCEPTION
```

Children are excellent recorders
of their experiences but poor interpreters.

— DAVID RIDDELL —

---

[40] *A More Excellent Way*: Pastor Henry Wright, 4th Edition 2000

CONCEPTION AND LIFE IN THE WOMB

A time to contemplate

After reading the first 18 verses of Psalm 139, do you feel you were unconditionally loved and accepted? Write down your own thoughts and feelings about being loved.

_____

_____

_____

_____

_____

_____

_____

_____

_____

_____

Chapter 7

PHYSICAL NEEDS, FEAR, GUILT AND SHAME

You may not remember all the events that have shaped your life, but you are certainly influenced by them. This may answer your struggle of why you can't always be who you want to be. You have an added problem; your body also has needs and desires. These desires are for warmth, food, liquids, sleep, recreation, procreation, touch etc. These are God-given desires and in themselves are healthy and normal. What might be iniquitous is how you fulfill these desires and what is driving them. What happens is that when you have a desire,[41] say for food, Satan can come and try to tempt you to fulfill your desires in the wrong way. The Holy Spirit, on the other hand, will help you fulfill those desires more appropriately.

Normally, as you grow up, your parents should teach you what is acceptable and unacceptable behaviour within your cultural context. This concept of what is right and wrong can also be looked at in terms of knowing good and evil.[42] Now the problem you may have is that

---
[41] James 1:13-15
[42] Genesis 2:17

PHYSICAL NEEDS, FEAR, GUILT AND SHAME

when you do something that you know is inappropriate or wrong, you feel guilty and because you are taught that wrong should be punished, you start to feel fear. you now begin to live under a cloud of fear, guilt, and shame. You will feel guilty when you have broken a rule or a law.

Here is an example:

Here is a fictious case of a young man in his twenties. He is at a party where there is plenty of delicious food. He is hungry and his body, through his subconscious mind, sends the message to his brain that he must eat. His emotions are aroused and tell him how nice the food is, adding to his natural, God-given desire. Unfortunately, this man grew up in poverty and as a child, there was never enough food to go around. This resulted in a fear of not having enough. His subconscious sends the message: "Here's your chance. Don't miss this opportunity." Before he realizes what is happening, he has overloaded his plate and overeaten. Because he knows this is inappropriate, he begins to feel guilty and is fearful of the consequences. The problem is that when he has repeated the same action several times, he may begin to live in fear of being unable to stop this behaviour.

Sometimes you may also experience feeling ashamed. Shame is a feeling you are a corrupt or bad person. Shame is often put on you by people, your culture and society.

Here is an example of how we can be shamed.

A little 3-year-old boy, named Jonny, is looking for some attention. His mum has some friends around for tea. So, he runs into the lounge and points to his ear and says, "ear". All the mums respond, "what a clever little boy!" Well, that works for the little chap. He runs into the lounge again and says "nose", pointing to his nose. Another round of applause. Jonny keeps running into the lounge, pointing to parts of his face, and getting attention he is looking for. Again, he runs into the lounge but has run out of ideas at what to point to. He pauses for a moment, whips down his pants, points to his penis, and says "willie". His mum is appalled and embarrassed. She picks him up and scolds him severely, "bad boy!". To Jonny it was just a body part. To his mum it meant something else. It is his mom's embarrassment and shame that is now imputed on to him.

There is an unfortunate consequence if you continually live under a cloud of fear, guilt, and shame. If you read verse 17 of Genesis 2, it states that when you know what is right or wrong, you will "surely die". The words for "surely die" in Hebrew means to 'die prematurely' or cause to die[43]. What happens is that when you begin to feel stressed because of fear, your hypothalamus gland, which controls the correct functioning your body, begins to malfunction[44]. This malfunctioning will eventually cause a breakdown of your health[45] and as a result you get sick and may eventually die earlier than was otherwise intended by God.

It has been scientifically verified that 75 to 98% of all mental health problems are caused by how we think.[46]

---

[43] Muth (Hebrew) – to die prematurely by neglect of wise moral conduct
[44] Principles of Anatomy & Physiology: Gerard J. Tortora & Nicholas P. Anagnostakos, 2nd Edition 1978
[45] A More Excellent Way: Pastor Henry Wright, 4th Edition 2000
[46] Switch on your Brain: Dr Caroline Leaf, 2015, page 37

PHYSICAL NEEDS, FEAR, GUILT AND SHAME

The diagram below shows the impact of your physical needs, guilt, and fear.

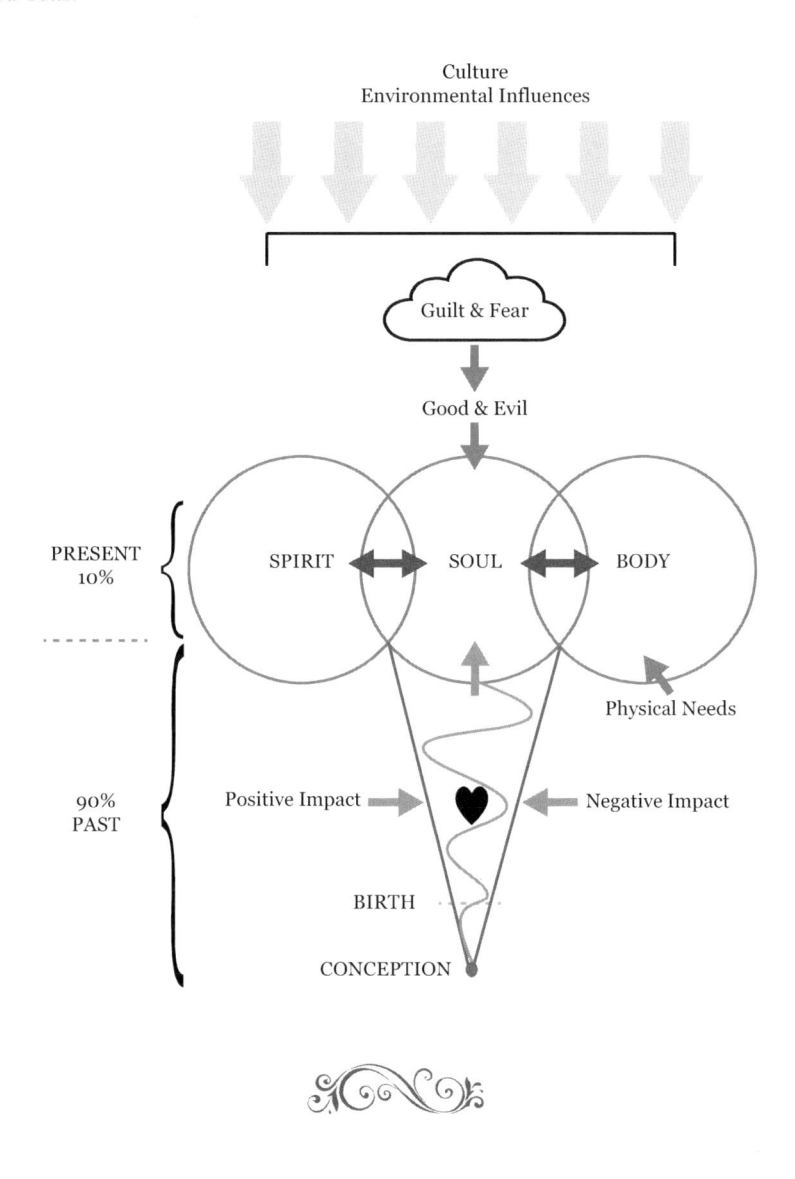

Diagram: Culture and Environmental Influences flow down into Guilt & Fear, then Good & Evil, affecting the Spirit–Soul–Body circles. Present = 10%, Past = 90%. Shows Positive Impact and Negative Impact converging on a heart between Conception and Birth, with Physical Needs acting on the Body.

Those who cannot remember the past are condemned to repeat it.

— GEORGE SANTAYANA —

39

A ROAD TO FREEDOM

A time to mull over

Write down one or two things that you do that causes you feel guilty.

_____
_____
_____

What 'rule' do you feel guilty about breaking?

_____
_____
_____

Who told you or where did you learn that breaking that 'rule' was wrong?

_____
_____
_____

What do you think the punishment will be for breaking that 'rule'?

_____
_____
_____

Chapter 8

SPIRITUAL ROOTS AND INFLUENCES

There is still one other area that you need to look at that can have a direct impact on how you behave. You are born into a broken world with generations of brokenness. This is a spiritual dynamic that can be observed through the effect it has upon your life. Without instruction, guidance and correction, children are instinctively curious and will do things that they know they should not be doing. Yet sometimes, despite all the instruction, guidance, and correction you have received, you simply continue to do the things that have detrimental consequences. Despite your best efforts, you may find you continually partake in unhelpful behaviors and actions. This may be due to spiritual influences.

Your soul is affected by sin, transgression, and iniquity. Let me briefly explain to you the differences between sin, transgression, and iniquity.

1. In the New Testament, the Greek word 'sin'[47] means to miss the mark, and so not share in life going smoothly. In simple terms it means you are doing things that God knows is unhelpful for you. It can range from

---

[47] hamartia (Greek)

A ROAD TO FREEDOM

some serious actions, like having sex with another man's wife, to ignoring the prompting of the Holy Spirit to phone a friend who is in need.

2   The word 'transgress'[48] in the New Testament means to act contrary to a command. (Here I am referring to natural and spiritual laws that govern the universe and not to the Mosaic laws of the Old Testament.) In terms of a natural law, let us discuss the law of gravity. Gravity works for every person on earth and if you ignore it by walking off the top of a building, you will suffer dire consequences. In a spiritual sense, you need to think about things like judgments,[49] sowing and reaping,[50] honouring your father and mother,[51] and unforgiveness.[52] These spiritual laws operate irrespective of whether you know about them or not and are not specific to any religion or belief system. When you transgress them there will be repercussions!

3   Iniquity[53] on the other hand is what you inherit from your previous generations. It implies that you are inclined to a specific course of action. This can be both useful or cause hardship and difficulties. It is like a rifle that has a bent barrel, you may aim correctly but are simply unable to hit the target. Typical areas of negative iniquity, passed down from generation to generation, may include divorce, sexual perversion, substance abuse, mental illness, health difficulties, poverty, and spiritual transference. There is strong scientific evidence that trauma is past down the generational line through your DNA[54].

The good news is that Jesus died for all your brokenness (sins, transgression, and iniquity) past, present and future. Unfortunately, this does not automatically make you impervious to the effects of your harmful actions or the effects passed down from your previous generations.

---

[48] parabaino (Greek)
[49] Matthew 7:1-2, Luke 6:37-38
[50] Galatians 6:7-8
[51] Ephesians 6:2-3
[52] Matthew 18:34-35
[53] Avon (Hebrew)
[54] https://www.psycom.net/epigenetics-trauma

SPIRITUAL ROOTS AND INFLUENCES

Here is a way of understanding iniquity:

Imagine you have a road where the speed limit is 30 miles per hour. This is a law of the country and if you are caught exceeding that speed limit, you can receive a fine. The reason that there is a speed limit on that road is for your own safety and for the safety of those around you. The local authority chooses to abolish that law. You are now able to travel at any speed on that road and cannot be punished if you excess 30 miles per hour. That the speed limit is abolished does not make the road any safer. So, you drive at a speed that is excessive and, as a result, have an accident, which will result in great loss and much pain. The legal authority cannot punish you because you have not broken any law. But you are affected by the consequences of your accident. This is not punishment but a consequence of your own actions! This is the same result when you do not keep to God's guidelines and have not dealt with iniquity.

Jesus set aside the law[55] when He established the New Covenant for you to live under. The result is that Father God in Heaven does not punish those who accept His offer of mercy. But you do bear the consequences of your actions here on earth. The good news is that Jesus also died for those consequences and can change the effect that those consequences have upon your life.

As you take a moment to consider all the things that affect you, it is no wonder you are not able to live to your full potential, nor can you expect others to be any different. If you go to the doctor, he might be able to heal your body, which will improve the condition of your soul and spirit, but it won't necessarily change your heart. You may go to a therapist, and this can help you change your thinking patterns. It can change how you are feeling emotionally and give you the necessary coping skills to make better decisions, but it seldom changes your heart. You may go to church, read your Bible, sing hymns, learn Scriptures and pray, but it still may not bring about the full desired effect of restoration.

---

[55] Romans 6:14

Likewise, what is in your heart, will produces a result in your life[56]. Interventions and coping skills are important, but unless the root is dealt with, the problem may reoccur or manifest itself in a different way.

Now that you have some idea of what makes you "tick", it is time to explore how you can be set free from the negative things of your past.

The diagram below shows the impact of generational iniquity.

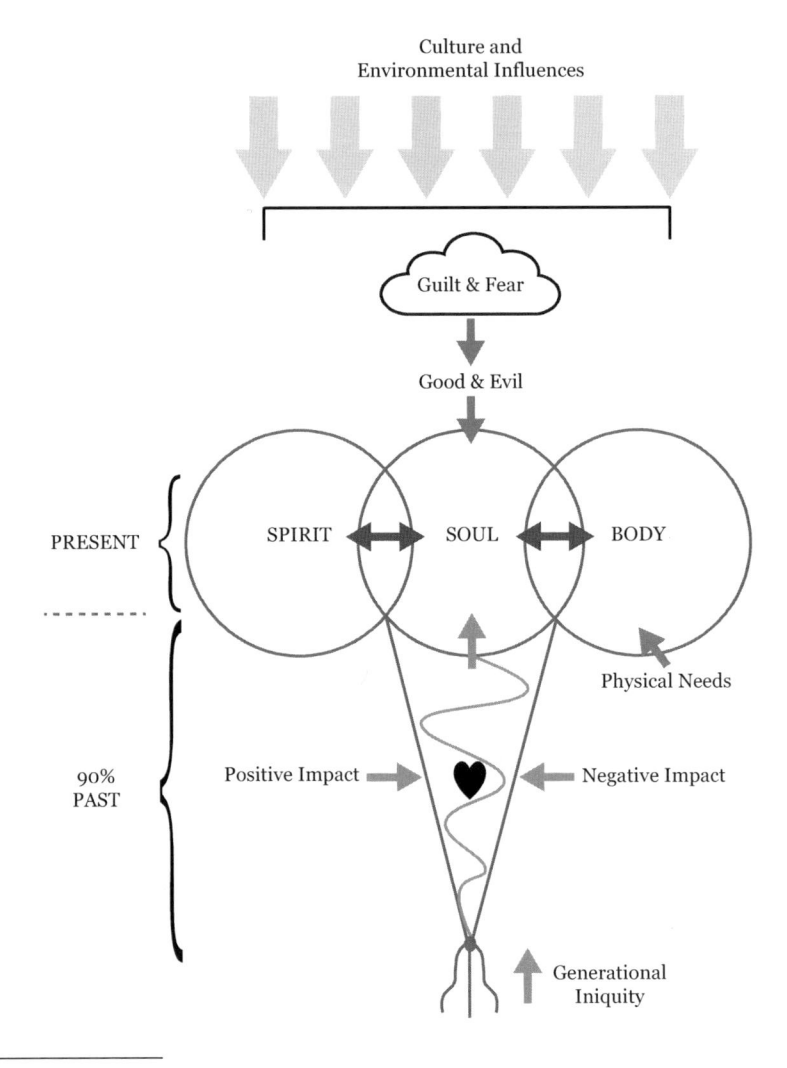

---

[56] Matthew 7:16-18

SPIRITUAL ROOTS AND INFLUENCES

*Jesus died for what we got wrong,
not for what we got right.*

— MERRIL —

A time to remember

Record any history of specific conditions, patterns or events that seem to re-occur in your previous generations.

_____

_____

Write down if any of your previous generations belonged to a cult, a sect, or secret organisation and how they are related to you.

_____

_____

Can you recall if there is anyone in your ancestry who pronounced curses, dabbled in the occult, or made pacts that are not beneficial? Record what you can remember.

_____

_____

If you have personally been involved in any of the above, briefly write down any details.

_____

_____

Chapter 9

A PLACE TO START

In Chapter 2 you learnt about 5 foundational principles for the restoration of your life so that you may become who the Father intended you to be. In looking at the process you need to understand that it is not your job to explore and look for what is wrong with you. It is the work of the Holy Spirit to show you the truth and direct your steps.[57] We are instructed to follow the Holy Spirit and live through Him.[58] This is very important because if you don't, you may only cause further unnecessary hardship.

Most of us are aware of several issues that may be causing us problems. Some of them may be severe, like an eating disorder, while other problems may be general dissatisfaction about an annoying habit. These problems, especially if you have struggled with them a long time, tend to make you feel hopeless, helpless, and unworthy. Because your self-image may be distorted, it is important to know how your Heavenly Father views, thinks and feels about you.

---

[57] John 16:13, Isaiah 30:21
[58] Galatians 5:16,18,25

Jesus died for your sins, transgressions, and iniquities. Therefore, there is no longer any punishment.[59] When the Heavenly Father looks at you, He sees you blameless and pure.[60] The Father sees who you were created to be at the same time knowing why you are unable to do life well.

The Heavenly Father loves you unconditionally.[61] If you spent the rest of your lives serving Him and living perfectly, the Heavenly Father could not love you more than He does right now. If you got nothing right, He would not love you any less! He loves you because you are His child.

When the Heavenly Father looks at you, He always sees you as you were created to be, not the way you are at this moment, and because of that, His heart of you does not change. You are unique and precious to Him. If the Heavenly Father lost you, He would lose the only one He ever created. There is no clone, no copy, and there is nothing that can replace you.

Think about this:

Imagine for a moment that you are holding in your hands a flawless diamond worth one billion pounds. If you put that diamond in a bucket of water, what is its value? Its value is still one billion pounds. Now you put that diamond in old dirty engine oil, what is its value? The value is still one billion pounds. What if you put that diamond in a block of concrete? What is its value then? Its value remains unchanged. Now if you put that diamond in the worst muck you can think of, has its value changed? No, the value of the diamond does not change irrespective of the stuff that is on it. Yes, it is dirty and therefore cannot reflect the light and sparkle or shine, but its value remains unchanged. In your Heavenly Father's eyes, you are that diamond and your value in His eyes does not change because of what has happened to you.

---

[59] Romans 5:1,5,18 and Romans 8:1
[60] John 15:3
[61] John 3:16, Jeremiah 31:3

A PLACE TO START

Only when you feel secure and safe can you be vulnerable enough to look at what is really in your heart.

In this world you are taught, from a very early age that you need to achieve, and that achievement means reward and acceptance. Just look at your schooling; you must study so that you can pass the examination and if you do not achieve a high enough mark you have failed. Unfortunately, you may have adopted the same approach to the kingdom of God. You may fear God's disapproval or rejection if you don't perform. This may result in you looking at the trials in your life as a series of tests set by God to see if you are good enough. This thinking is false. Your Heavenly Father knows everything about you.[62] He knows what is is broken or what pressure or strain something can take before it breaks. He does not have to test you to find out; He already knows.

Picture this:

*Suppose I have a table with a broken leg. I love that table, and I know that it can still balance if I don't put any weight on the broken leg. So, I use the table by putting things on the table over the 3 good legs. It is working wonderfully. You are visiting me, and I am very excited about your visit. I come in with a tray of tea, coffee, milk, sugar, and biscuits. In my excitement, I put the tray down on the table over the broken leg. The table collapses and there is tea, coffee, milk, sugar, and biscuits all over the floor. Can I be cross with the table? I knew it could not take the weight, so I cannot blame the table. This is the same with your Heavenly Father. To Him, you are like that table. He knows where your broken "legs" are. He is not caught out when the events of life cause you to "collapse", where your weaknesses are. When He allows the events of life to come upon you, and you "collapse" He is **not** trying to catch you out. What He is revealing to you is the brokenness in you, that He wants to heal so that you can live life abundantly. What He wants, is for you to come to Him so that He can restore you. The reason He wants you to be*

---

[62] Hebrews 4:13, 1 John 3:20, Psalm 139:4

whole is so that you can enjoy life. He is never disappointed when you "collapse" because He already knows. What He is disappointed with, is when you won't come to Him to be healed and be restored or when you try to fix it yourself. He wants you to come to the "carpenter" Jesus, and have a "new leg" made and fitted to your "table". Then you can never "collapse" under the pressures of life!

So, how do you know when the Holy Spirit is trying to reveal an issue to you? Obviously, you may know if you have a specific problem, an illness or mental health problem. These are outward signs of something a lot deeper. I would like to suggest that you say to your Heavenly Father, "I have a problem with *(the problem)*. Please show me why I am struggling with this." Now just continue with life and don't try to 'hear' an answer. For the rest of the day just notice your emotions and responses to events. When you become aware of your reaction, ask yourself, "Is your response love, joy, peace, patience, kindness, goodness, faithfulness, gentleness, or self-control with perseverance?"[63] If it is not one of the fruits of the Holy Spirit, then it is probably not useful in your life. If it is not useful and causing you unpleasantness, then, I suggest, get rid of it. This is the Holy Spirit putting His finger on that which He wants to restore. Follow me, and in the following chapters I will show you how "to get rid of it".

You cannot surrender yourself to something you don't know or don't trust.

— JOHN COLES —

---

[63] Galatians 5:22-23

A PLACE TO START

A time to give consideration to...

Write down any unpleasant feelings[64] caused by something or what someone said or did.

_____

_____

Write down how often these feelings seem to occur.

_____

_____

What sort of reactions do you think you would like to have, rather than these feelings and reactions?

_____

_____

Is there something the Holy Spirit has been talking to you about right now?

_____

_____

---

[64] See list of unpleasant feeling words to help you in Appendix 3.

Chapter 10

EMOTIONAL RESTORATION

We are going to discuss three simple steps that can help you on the road to your restoration. These are confession, forgiveness, and cancelling the debt. You may know these words but often they are not fully understood or correctly applied.

CONFESSION:

Confession is acknowledging that you have a problem and secondly that you accept that you are responsible for your own emotions and behaviour. People are often very quick to blame others or God for the way they feel and while you do this, you will not find freedom. The circumstances may be beyond your control but in the end, you still have the free will to choose how you are going to deal with the situation. We have the example of Jesus in the Gospels, of how he reacted when they mocked and spat on him.[65] There is nothing written there that indicates that he accused his persecutors or defended his position. My understanding of his ability to react so differently, compared to

---

[65] Matthew 27:28-31, Mark 15:18-20

myself, was that he had no unresolved issues and consequently, he was able to react *(his free will choice)* with compassion and forgiveness.[66]

It is extremely beneficial if you can talk confidentially to another person whom you can trust, about what has happened to you and how you feel as a result. This talking[67] will generally initiate catharsis[68], and is part of the confession process. If there are tears or weeping, try not hold it back; God never intended you to internalise pain. Even Jesus wept.[69]

The Bible says, and I suggest that you pray aloud, you need to acknowledge your feelings, that you have missed the mark (sinned) and that you want Christ to change you on the inside.[70] I have included a list of 'negative feeling' words to help identify your emotions in the appendix[71] that you may find helpful.

FORGIVENESS:

Forgiveness is central to the New Covenant. It is very clear that you must forgive those that have offended and hurt you. You have been forgiven much and so in the same way you need to be forgiving.[72] But simply saying, "I forgive you" is not enough, since this does not change the hurt or pain, you may be feeling. True forgiveness will change the emotional impact of the situation and for that to happen you need to forgive from the heart. The most significant aspect of forgiveness is that it frees you and therefore, if you don't forgive, you are trapped.[73]

Let us examine what forgiveness is and what it is not.

---

[66] Luke 23:34
[67] 1 John 1:9
[68] On Becoming a Person - Carl R. Rogers – 1961
[69] John 11:35
[70] See Appendix 2 for a sample Confession prayer
[71] See Appendix 3
[72] Matthew 18:23-33
[73] Matthew 18:34 -35

To begin with, let us look at those Roman soldiers who tortured and mocked Jesus, who drove the nails into Jesus' hands and feet and crucified Him. If those Roman soldiers really, really knew who Jesus was and loved like He loved them, would they have done it? Somehow, I think not. Jesus knew that they didn't recognize who He was nor grasped what they were doing. That is why He was able to say, "*Father, forgive them. They **don't know** what they are doing.*"[74] Forgiveness is an understanding that people don't realise the impact of their actions, what they are saying, what they are doing, nor do they comprehend the consequences. We are all broken people, born into a broken world with all types of sin and iniquity, with all types of hurts and traumas and you are incapable of doing the right thing all the time.

Forgiveness does not mean that a person's wrong actions or behaviour is acceptable or that you can allow the pattern to continue.

Here is a case study:

I was counselling a woman whose husband was physically abusing her. I suggest to the wife, "It may help you if you forgive your husband." She looked at me and said, "You must be joking!" The reason may have been that she thinks by forgiving him, she is accepting that what he did is okay and that it gave him permission to continue. This is not forgiveness. This abusive behaviour is not acceptable and maybe a restraining order was necessary, or police assistance needed to be sought. His behaviour was inappropriate, and he needed help. Here we were not rejecting him but restraining him until he realised, he needed help.

Forgiveness has nothing to do with who has done what, who is right and who is wrong. Forgiveness does not depend upon the person that hurt you. Forgiveness has everything to do with the hurt you are experiencing, and you being set free.

Another case study:

---

[74] Luke 23:34

EMOTIONAL RESTORATION

I counselled a woman who was molested as a child. I suggest to her that it would help her if she forgave the perpetrator. She responded by saying, "Why should I forgive? I didn't do anything wrong." Absolutely true, she didn't do anything wrong. She was an innocent child. I then asked her, "If the molester went to Jesus and asked Jesus to forgive him, would Jesus forgive him?" Obviously, the answer was yes. I then asked her to consider the following: "Jesus did not do anything wrong either. If Jesus is prepared to forgive him and then maybe this is something you should consider too?"

Forgiveness does not imply that you need to become buddies with the person that hurt you.[75] You cannot be at peace with another person while they are unrepentant. There is a big difference between forgiveness and being reconciled. Reconciliation requires an action from both parties whereas forgiveness is all about you, setting yourself free.

Here are a couple of questions that you could ask yourselves when you felt hurt by someone:

- If they really, really knew how their actions hurt you, would they have done it?
- If they really, really were able to love me as Jesus loves you, would they have said that?
- Did they get up this morning with the intention of doing something to upset you?
- If they intentionally intended to hurt someone, consider what hurt they must have suffered that they have no love or concern for others?

You can say the words, "I forgive you", and be very honest about it, but how do you do it from the heart? The only way you can forgive from the heart is through the help of the Holy Spirit. That is why the Holy Spirit is your counsellor.[76]

---

[75] Romans 12:18
[76] John 14:16, 26

We will discuss two methods you can use to engage with the Holy Spirit to help you. In both instances it is more helpful if you are in a secure quiet place where you will not be disturbed and there are no distractions. If you find the quietness a bit intimidating, you could softly play some background music that has no singing to fill the space.

Method 1: I suggest you speak out loud, saying, "Heavenly Father, you require that I should forgive (name) from my heart. I cannot do this, and so I need your help. Please send your Holy Spirit to help me. Holy Spirit please put me in the shoes of (name) who hurt me so that I may understand why they did what they did and what motivated them." Now quietly focus on the Holy Spirit. Sometimes within minutes you will receive a revelation of what motivated that person. Other times it may take a lot longer. The point is you don't struggle to get an answer as the Holy Spirit flows with inspiration. Sometimes the Holy Spirit may only give you the revelation a couple of days later or through a dream. The point is that if you keep asking, you will get an answer.[77]

Method 2: Sometimes, due to the emotional pain you are experiencing, it is very difficult to focus quietly on the Holy Spirit. Here it may be helpful to just focus on the emotional pain. As you do this, you may begin to discover deeper levels or sources of the pain, alternatively you may recall previous incidents where you have experienced similar events or hurts. Quietly ask the Holy Spirit to be with you as these events surface and reveal to you what caused these people to do these things. Again, allow the Holy Spirit to bring his revelation in his own time.

Last case study:

I was counselling a man in his thirties. His current problem was that he was unable to hold down a job. Invariably, he would disappear and drink himself into a stupor. We had worked through several other issues, when one day he recounted how he had an emotional breakdown while training to

---

[77] Matthew 7:7-8

become a chef. He felt that Master Chef was particularly hard and abusive towards him. He agreed when I suggested he should forgive Master Chef. I suggested he close his eyes and ask the Holy Spirit to help him to forgive by 'putting him in Master Chef's shoes'".

It was less than 3 minutes when he opened his eyes and began repeatedly blurting out, "He loves me!" After a while he told me that the Holy Spirit showed him that Master Chef considered himself a failure and because Master Chef 'loved' him, he didn't want him also to become a failure. Master Chef didn't know any other way of training except by being harsh and demanding. I asked my client, "Can you forgive Master Chef?" He looked at me smiling and said, "I have already forgiven him, from the bottom of my heart!"

The process of forgiveness described here is not about trying to recall memories or trying to re-experience the past. It is about seeing the unpleasant events from God's perspective. When you see things from God's perspective, you realise that your perceptions are usually false. The revelation of your error-based thinking helps you to be released from the pain associated with the event. Your pain and emotional hurts are rooted in your interpretation of the event and not in the event itself.[78] [79]

FORGIVING OURSELVES:

It is far easier to forgive others than it is to forgive ourselves. You have probably chided yourself with "I should have known better" or "I should have chosen differently". The fact is, at the that time, you were not able to do it differently. If you had a different understanding or more information then or better life skills, you might have chosen differently but you could not. With different information you may have been able to make different choices. Also, if there are unresolved

---

[78] Healing Life's Hurts through Theophostic Prayer: Edward M Smith – 2005
[79] See Appendix 2 for a sample Forgiveness prayer.

emotional experiences from the past, and these had been dealt with, then maybe, you could have done it differently. It is a well-researched understanding that the unresolved hurts and pain from the past will cause you to act differently to the way you want to or would like to. This is because of your lower brain which responds automatically; but more about this later.

What you must realise is that when you have accepted Jesus as your Lord and Savior, your spirit person became something completely new[80], that did not previously exist. Your soul and body have not become something new, only your spirit. Your spirit is now in Christ Jesus[81] and Jesus is seated in the heavenly realms at the right hand of the Father[82]. So, your spirit is in the heavenly realm, but your soul and body are still here on earth. As we discussed earlier, it is this part that still carries all the hurts and brokenness of the past. So, part of you is perfect and part of you is still needing restoration. Think about it this way; we have a brilliant skilled driver in a rattletrap of a car. The car keeps breaking down or keeps veering off the road. Is the problem with the driver or the car? It is the car that is broken, but you, as the "driver", have the responsibility to get the car repaired.

If you are not willing to forgive yourself, then you are saying that your standard is better than God's standard. When you received Jesus as your Lord and saviour, all your sins, past, present, and future are forgiven. But then, you need to forgive yourself.

So how do you do this? Seat yourself in the spirit realm and talk to that part of you which is still on earth, your soul. You address your soul as you would speaking to another person using your own name[83].

---

[80] 2 Corinthians 5:17
[81] 1 Corinthians 1:30
[82] Mark 16:19
[83] See Appendix 2 for a sample "Forgiving yourself" prayer

CANCELING THE DEBT:

In the book of Matthew, you have a passage of scripture, which is known as the Lord's Prayer. There you read that you are exhorted to forgive your 'debtors' in the same manner that you can ask the Lord to forgive your 'debts'. This word 'debts' has often been substituted with the words 'sin' or 'transgression'.[84] The word 'debt'[85] means something owed or due and comes from a root word meaning to be under obligation or having morally failed in duty. A 'debt' is often experienced as resentment that you retain within your heart resulting from unmet expectations; in other words, "you should have acted differently towards me; now you owe me."

Unfortunately, when your expectations are not met you may judge that person,[86] which in turn impacts on your own life. It is like when a stone is thrown into a pond; the ripples first go outwards, hit the bank, and then return to the source. The result is that you may harbour judgmental attitudes, which result in unkind responses. You are now involved with what the Bible calls 'sowing and reaping'.[87] If these behaviours are directed towards your parents, you start failing to 'honour your parents'.[88] These are all transgressions of immutable spiritual laws that apply to everybody[89] and could result in a root of bitterness within your heart. What becomes even more of a problem is that this bitterness may cause others to act towards you in an unpleasant manner,[90] opposite to what you want or expect.

It is relatively easy to know if you have a debt in your heart by how you may avoid somebody or feel anger towards a person. Typically, you may be walking in town when you see someone coming along

---

[84] See Chapter 8 where the words 'sin' and 'transgress' are discussed.
[85] Opheilema (Greek)
[86] Matthew 7:1-2, Luke 6:37-38
[87] Galatians 6:7-8
[88] Ephesians 6:2-3
[89] Matthew 5:45
[90] Hebrews 12:15

that you don't want to speak to and so the sale on the other side of the road suddenly becomes more appealing.

The question we now need to answer is how do you go about getting rid of the resentment you have inside of you, because of how somebody treated you?

A story:

When I was still a lad, my father reprimanded me for something I did not do. As much as I tried to explain my side of the story, dad would not listen which was the least I

expected from him. I now harbour resentment toward him as he should have listened; in other words, 'dad, you owe me'. The problem that now it seems to re-occur in my life, is that authority figures never seem to listen to me. Ugh!

The only way you can get rid of this type of resentment is if you go to your Heavenly Father who truly understands and can console you. My suggestion is that you should ask your Heavenly Father to forgive you for your judgments and offense you feel towards that person, for them not doing what you needed and expected. When you cancel the debt and forgive them, you will find that you no longer become upset with that person when they are unable to treat you correctly,[91] because you know, your Heavenly Father has promised to provide all your needs[92] and do what is right for you.

The above suggestion may not work out the way you may want, and that is because every person and every situation are different. You are unique and your Heavenly Father can do things differently. What is of importance is that you understand the principals involved and that it is the Heavenly Father who does the work of restoration.

---

[91] See Appendix 2 for a sample Cancelling the Debt prayer
[92] Philippians 4:19

Finally, a word of caution: you may have emotional wounds, which may have resulted in you creating ways of coping so that you don't feel the pain. As you begin this process of restoration, your protective mechanisms are going to be dismantled, which will result in you being even more sensitive and aware of your wounding. Because you are more sensitive, this does not mean you are not getting better, but rather, that restoration is taking place in your life and that you are being made whole, which will result in you are more aware of your brokenness and negative emotions.

An example:

When you are hurt by the events of life, you build walls or put on pieces of armour to protect that sensitive area. The result is that you don't feel the sticks and stones that life or people throw at you. But the moment the walls comes down or your defensiveness is lessened you have less protection, and the smallest things now seem to hurt.

A greater awareness of your emotional pain may also indicate that further restoration is required. With the help of the Holy Spirit, you continue the process of confession, forgiveness and canceling the debt. As you are restored and healed, you need to develop different skills and approaches to handling situations. This process is called the 'renewing of your mind' or a new way of thinking,[93] and we will share more about this in the next chapter.

*Judgments occur when we have an expectation
regarding the performance of a person
and those expectations are not met.*

— Merril —

---

[93] Romans 12:2

A ROAD TO FREEDOM

A time to give space for the Holy Spirit

At the end of the previous chapter, you were asked several questions. Review your answers and with the help of the Holy Spirit begin to confess, forgive, and cancel the debts.

Chapter 11

RENEWING THE MIND - REPENTANCE

As we together look at repentance, we need to move beyond the Biblical Hebrew context of just returning to the Lord with sorrow and being spared from God's judgment. Repentance[94] under the New Covenant is having a new insight on an issue and because of a different understanding, you can choose to think, act, and behave differently. It is like, having lived your life one way, you then make a U-turn and start living differently.

The most remarkable change of perspective occurs when the Holy Spirit brings a revelation on a specific event or subject. The revelation is so impressive that in an instant this changes your attitude, emotions, and behaviour. But at other times that change may take a little longer, requiring purposeful decisions and positive actions.

REPENTANCE AND NEURAL PATHWAYS:

Neuro-science research has shown that the brain develops neural-pathways. All thoughts are generated in the brain and flow along a path

---

[94] metanoia (Greek)

from neuron to neuron and through repetition this becomes an automatic process. An example of this is riding a bicycle. Positive thoughts create a positive reaction in the body. Laughter will activate endorphins which cause the body to be healed, while, anger and rage, will produce chemicals and hormones that are destructive to your body.[95]

Fortunately, these pathways can be changed and is referred to as neuroplasticity which is the ability of the brain to create new and different neural connections[96].

Clearly it is important to be changed by thinking correctly. The bible encourages and supports the impact of thinking and its effects upon the body and the soul.[97]

REPENTANCE AND THOUGHT PATTERNS:

Let us now consider how thinking patterns are formed. When you were born, you had no idea how to live in the world, in your macro and micro cultures. In the frontal lobes of your neocortex, your upper brain, are mirror neurons. These mirror neurons help you to tune into the emotional states and intensions of another person.[98] As a baby, your brain connects and mimics your mother and later on you mimic others around you. The brain is influenced by both positive and negative emotions of those around you. Unknowingly you are drawn into a way of thinking, a thought pattern, that when repeated sufficiently, will become a default way of thinking or a neural pathway. This process can occur through your whole life.

The thought patterns result in physical responses in your body and behavioural patterns. These natural habit sequences can help you fulfill many routine tasks that are essential for living, for example like

---

[95] Healing Begins with the Sanctification of the Heart 'No Disease is Incurable' Dr MK Strydom, Second Edition 2010
[96] See www.medicinenet.com for a medical definition of neuroplasticity
[97] Proverbs 17:22 and 23:7, Romans 12:2, Philippians 4:8, 3 John vs 2
[98] The Body Keeps the Score – Bessel van der Kolk, 2015, p 58, 59

RENEWING THE MIND - REPENTANCE

brushing your teeth. Unfortunately, due to negative events, beyond your control, you can also develop some unhealthy and debilitating thinking patterns and habits, which after a time, becomes an automatic response which you cannot seem to change or get rid of.

Here is an example:

Let us say that I grew up in a house where the door of my bedroom jammed against the floor when the door was opened halfway. After a while I learnt to open the door to a point just before it became stuck. This was so practiced that I would subconsciously open the door the correct amount even while thinking about something else.

Then one day, after 20 years, somebody came along and sanded the bottom of the door so that the door could now open fully. When I came into my room, I still subconsciously opened the door halfway. Only when I was through the doorway did I realise that the door was repaired. So, I now have to re-program myself to think and react differently. After about a month or so of practice, I start to create a new automatic response.

The simplest way of changing an annoying thinking pattern and habit is by asking the Holy Spirit to remind you and then consciously do something different. For example, if you are critical[99] or bad-mouthed you can change by asking the Holy Spirit to help you speak differently.[100] Sometimes you only remember moments after you have repeated the habit. When this happens, you acknowledge that this is a process, and you repeat the steps you are implementing to change. What you must not do is criticize yourselves. What may be more useful, is to say, "Thank you Lord for your forgiveness and grace. Holy Spirit continue to change me."[101] You also need to apologise (again) and ask forgiveness if you have offended someone. At no time do you allow self-criticism or think that you must try harder or that you are not

---
[99] Ephesians 4:29
[100] See Appendix 2 for a sample Repentance prayer
[101] Palm 51:10

forgiven. This will only lead to a downward spiral of self-effort and self-effort which nullifies[102] the work of the Holy Spirit. This now becomes an act of faith in God that He can complete the process.[103]

Another way to help your brain develop a different neural pathway, is to repeat a phase or a positive mantra. One method is to repeat it 20 times, without a pause. This is repeated daily. This stops the brain from encountering the old thought pattern. This work, called "Re-wire Your Brain"[104] was developed by Dr. Genevieve Milnes.

REPENTANCE AND UN-RESOLVED ISSUES:

Sometimes it may happen that you have experienced a remarkable insight on an issue through the Holy Spirit, but when faced with a similar situation you react with negative emotions. It may simply mean that there is a deeper work or another situation that needs to be addressed. Simply go and repeat the process[105] as outlined in Chapter 10. The original event has been dealt with through confession and forgiveness and therefore does not need to be repeated. This process may take a while to complete, but it certainly becomes easier, and life will become more enjoyable each time[106] you deal with a hurt.

REPENTANCE AND RESOLVED ISSUES:

You may have a fear of confrontation with an authority figure and after having applied confession, forgiveness etc., you may find yourselves in a similar situation again. Your initial reaction may be that you do not want to face this person and are questioning, why it is happening all over again? There may be several reasons why you may be confronted

---

[102] Isaiah 64:6, John 15:4-5
[103] Philippians 1:6
[104] http://psychaust.com.au/rewiring/4594224761
[105] Philippians 2:12
[106] 2 Corinthians 3:18

by a similar or identical situation. By being in that situation again you may realise that you are healed, that you are able to react differently and that you don't have to fear that person or situation. I personally believe that it is not the Heavenly Father testing you but rather Him showing you that you are able to overcome all situations. Here your minds are being renewed to the fact that you are renewed!

CONCLUSION:

Today, science is proving what the Scriptures have always said, that you can be more than conquerors and that you can gain surpassing victory[107]. Your mind and thinking is more powerful than you have ever realized[108]. You can change if you choose, but you must choose. Once you have chosen, all of heaven's resources are available to you. You need to stop blaming your genes, your circumstances, or your upbringing. Yes, they were instrumental to where you are now, but now is the time to grasp the future God has for you.

*Nothing in the Kingdom comes cheap, although it is all free.
Everything must be intensely desired so that every idol
and stumbling block in the way is destroyed.*

— MERRIL —

---

[107] 2 Corinthians 3:18
[108] Recommended Reading: "Switch on your brain" Dr. Caroline Leaf

A ROAD TO FREEDOM

A time to ask...

(Write your impressions as you wait upon the Holy Spirit.)

Lord, is there anything, in the way I am living, that is displeasing to you?

_____

_____

_____

Lord, is there anything, in the way I am thinking, that is displeasing to you?

_____

_____

_____

Lord, is there anything, in the way I am speaking, that is displeasing to you?

_____

_____

_____

Part 2

SPIRITUAL RESTORATION

Chapter 12

UNDERSTANDING THE SPIRITUAL KINGDOMS

In chapters 3 and 8, we briefly talked about the fact that we are spirit, soul, and body and that we have roots of iniquity. We will now take a deeper look at the spiritual component.

Generally, western society places more importance on the intellect than on the spiritual. The reason for this is that it is difficult to prove the things of the spiritual realm[109] scientifically. There are two ways that you may understand the spiritual realm more, and that is by believing the stories of others or by experiencing it yourself. This immediately leaves you with two problems. Firstly, you are inclined to disregard your own personal spiritual experiences as a figment of your imagination especially when others discredit your experiences. Secondly, there are two spiritual kingdoms,[110] and unfortunately the kingdom of Satan will often try to pass itself off as 'good'[111] and will even draw you in by appearing beneficial, often appealing to your ego.

---
[109] 1 Corinthians 2:14
[110] Colossians 1:13, 2 Timothy 4:18
[111] 2 Corinthians 11:13-15

There are some other aspects of the spiritual world that you should also think about. It is a place where all is revealed and where good and evil are separated.[112] It is a place where you were created and to which we shall all return when our temporary earthly experiences are over.[113] In that spiritual world you will know Father God and worship will spontaneously flow from you. While you live in an earthly body the spiritual world is, for the most part, hidden from you.[114] But while we live on earth, we have a unique privilege. We have a free will. This world is the one place where you can choose to worship or not worship God. Here on earth, we are not overwhelmed by His beauty and His majesty, and you are not compelled to worship Him. It is through your love and worship of Him here on earth, that the Father is blessed.

We also need to be able to discern the differences between the kingdom of God, which is good, and the kingdom of Satan, which is lies[115] and deceit.[116]

Most things have a spiritual component and whenever you consider anything, you should first examine its content and if possible, what the original source or motivation is. Secondly, you need to examine the fruit and the results that it will eventually have in your life.

The below table will help you to understand the differences between the two spiritual kingdoms. By having a good discernment of the differences, you should be able to avoid being drawn into something that could harm you.

---

[112] Luke 16:23-26
[113] Ecclesiastes 12:7
[114] I Corinthians 13:12
[115] John 8:44
[116] Acts 13:10

	KINGDOM OF GOD CONTENT & MOTIVATION	KINGDOM OF SATAN CONTENT & MOTIVATION
1	ACCEPTS TESTING	DOES NOT LIKE TO BE TESTED
2	COMFORTING	FEARFUL
3	CONFORMS TO GOD'S NATURE	VIOLATES GOD'S NATURE
4	CONFORMS TO SCRIPTURE	USES SCRIPTURE OUT OF CONTEXT
5	GENDERS HUMILITY	APPEALS TO EGO
6	INSTRUCTIVE	CONFUSING
7	IT IS HONEST	ALTERS SCRIPTURE TO SUIT ITSELF
8	FREEING	MANIPULATIVE
9	NON-SECRETIVE	SECRETIVE
10	POSITIVE	NEGATIVE
11	CONSTRUCTIVE	DESTRUCTIVE
	FRUIT & RESULT	**FRUIT & RESULT**
1	ALLOWS GRACEFUL ACCEPTANCE	BRINGS CONDEMNATION
2	BRINGS CONVICTION	BRINGS DOUBT
3	BRINGS FREEDOM	BRINGS BONDAGE
4	BRINGS ENLIGHTENMENT	BRINGS CONFUSION
5	EMPOWERS & STRENGTHENS	BRINGS COMPULSION & DRIVES
6	SHOWS HUMILITY	EGOTISTICAL
7	BRINGS PEACE	DISTURBED FEELINGS
8	BRINGS POSITIVE EMOTIONS	BRINGS NEGATIVE EMOTIONS
9	QUICKENS FAITH	FEARFUL
10	TRUTHFUL & HONEST	DISHONEST & SCHEMING
11	TEACHABLE & SUBMISSIVE	STUBBORN & UN-SUBMISSIVE

As believers of the New Covenant, you are encouraged to give emphasis to the spiritual aspects of your life. In Galatians you are urged to live, walk, and be led[117] by the Holy Spirit. The Holy Spirit is your constant companion[118] who will teach and remind you[119] of everything. He is your guide[120],

---

[117] Galatians 5:16,18,25
[118] John 14:17-18
[119] John 14:26
[120] John 16:13

and He will direct you[121]. God can communicate with you though several different ways but for now we will consider how you are able to live being directed by the Holy Spirit. Jesus said you can hear him speak to you[122] and you need to choose to believe it. You also need to understand that He communicates with you through your spirit[123] by means of a spontaneous flow of thoughts or pictures from your spirit into your mind.

Understand it this way:

When you speak, you make a sound that is picked up by your ears. The resulting air vibration is transferred to your brain interpreting the impulses into meaningful words. When God speaks to you, the message comes into your mind, via your spirit and then into your brain as a thought or a mental picture. Your problem is that you usually dismiss these thoughts because they appear to be random or spontaneous and contrary to logic. More often, these random, spontaneous thoughts may be completely different to what you were thinking about at the moment.

You may be working when unexpectedly, a thought or a picture of somebody you know comes into your mind. This may be the Holy Spirit prompting you to pray or do something for them. Using the above table on content and motivation, you can check if it is from God or not. When God speaks to you in this way, it may defy your logical reasoning and Satan will try to get you dismiss to it as nonsense. As an example, you may be prompted to give a gift to someone who is obnoxious. You are now on a walk of faith, an exciting adventure, as you do not know how it will turn out. Sometimes you may only see the result of your actions months or even years later, if at all.

---

[121] Isaiah 30:21
[122] John 10:3 and 27
[123] I Corinthians 2:10-12

A ROAD TO FREEDOM

A time to inspect content and fruit

Write down a time when you felt prompted to take an unusual course of action.

_____
_____
_____

Reflecting on that event, consider the content and motivation using the above table in this chapter.

_____
_____
_____

Reflecting on that event consider the fruit and the result.

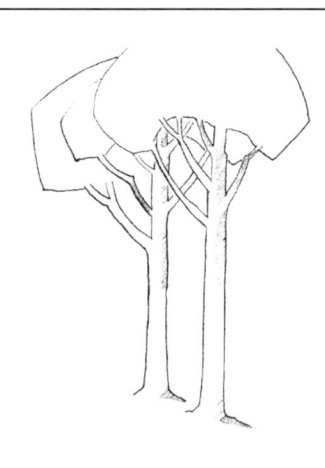

_____
_____
_____

Chapter 13

TACTICS, SOUL TIES & STRONGHOLDS

Before the establishment of the New Covenant, Satan ruled over the kingdoms of the world, and when he offered Jesus all the kingdoms of the world with their authority and glory[124], he was not joking. Satan gained control over the kingdoms of the earth when Adam and Eve defaulted, but when Jesus died on the cross a dramatic change occurred regarding the kingdom of darkness. Scripture refers to three specific areas of change to the kingdom of evil. Firstly, Jesus took away the weapons[125] that the kingdom of darkness was able to use against you. This was done openly and not in secret. Secondly, Jesus caused the kingdom of darkness to become inactive, inoperative and idle[126], and thirdly, Jesus also loosened and freed that which the devil had held captive and everything else that he was engaged with.[127]

---

[124] Matthew 4:8-9, Luke 4:5-7
[125] Colossians 2:15
[126] Hebrews 2:14
[127] 1 John 3:8(b)

Having understood that Satan is already defeated you need to understand how he is able to maintain some control over you. You can be manipulated through deception, slander, and misinformation. Once Satan knows that you have believed the lie, you become trapped and for all intents and purposes, it may as well be true. Let us now look and understand the devil's tactics.

DECEPTION:

Jesus described the devil as a liar[128] and said that there is not a single ounce of truth in what he says. Satan will therefore attack your self-image and self-worth. The devil will tell you, that you are worthless, unworthy, and will humiliate you in every way possible. If you get your values from the world then you are controlled by what the world thinks, and the kingdom of darkness likes to be in control of the world and all the pleasures and power it offers. Therefore, it is vital for you to know who you are in Christ. Satan's accusations are always general and are non-specific. Satan will question God's truth by asking, "Did God really say…?"[129] or he will misuse Scripture to deceive you into wrong thinking and bad choices. He tried this tactic on Jesus after Jesus had been fasting for 40 days.[130]

The Holy Spirit is always specific about what is inappropriate and will always point you to Jesus. It is imperative that you know what the Heavenly Father thinks about you, as this will protect your heart.[131] When you become aware you are being deceived, the best tactic is to speak out aloud God's truth[132] regarding yourself, in a similar manner as Jesus did during his temptation.[133]

---

[128] John 8:44
[129] Genesis 3:1
[130] Matthew 4:3-10
[131] Proverbs 4:23
[132] Isaiah 59:21, Ephesians 6:17
[133] Luke 4:3-12

SLANDER & GOSSIP:

We are told that the devil makes accusations[134] against those who believe Jesus is the Son of God. You will need to constantly remind yourself that when you accepted Jesus as your Lord, the Holy Spirit came to live inside of you,[135] and in living through God's spirit,[136] you are able to be like Christ. When you become critical and judgmental of other believers,[137] you become the devil's instrument of accusation. Satan uses gossip and slander spoken by people to discredit believers and create division and distrust. Once trust is broken, you are no longer able to live in unity[138] and as a result you begin to hide your true feelings.[139] When you become an instrument of gossip and slander you grieve the Holy Spirit[140] who lives inside of you and as result you also begin to suffer.

INTIMIDATION:

If Satan can get you to believe that he is more powerful than Christ in you, you will tend to capitulate. Because you have become immobilized and powerless, the devil is then able to rob, kill and destroy.[141]

Consider this scenario:

A young lad, 13 years of age, walks into a shop and sticks a gun into the ribs of the man behind the till. The man fearing for his life gives the young lad the money in the till. Later when the young lad is caught, it is found that the gun was only a toy. What do you think would have been the man's reaction if, at the time of the robbery, he had known the gun was only a toy?

---

[134] Revelation 12:10
[135] I Corinthians 3:16, Ephesians 1:13
[136] Ephesians 3:16-17
[137] Romans 14:4
[138] I Corinthians 12:12
[139] 1 John 1:7
[140] Ephesians 4:25-30
[141] John 10:10

This is what the devil tries to do with you. You hear and believe stories, which brings you into fear[142] and you begin to feel intimidated and powerless.

ERRONEOUS THINKING:

Erroneous thinking or believing something that is false is the most powerful, debilitating and controlling tactic of Satan[143] that can keep you trapped in unbelief.

Here is an illustration:

You are wearing spectacles that have red lenses. I hold up a piece of white paper. What colour does the paper appear to you? In your brain, it will appear to you as red, which is true. But the truth is it is white. Now imagine that from the first moment you could see, you wore red spectacles, you would not believe me if I told you that the paper was white. In fact, you would not even know what white is. I would not be able to convince you because you know what you are seeing. The only way you could know the truth is if somebody removed the red spectacles.

This is the difference between what is true and truth. What you think, believe or experience may be true but may not necessarily be the truth. Jesus said the result would be according to the way you believe.[144] Fear is triggered by unbelief. Unbelief is the opposite of faith. Therefore, if you know and believe the truth you can walk in faith.

THE IMPLICATION OF SOUL TIES:

We learn about soul ties from the Scriptures where we read that the soul of Jonathan was joined to the soul of David.[145] This occurred

---

[142] 1 Peter 5:8
[143] 2 Timothy 2:26
[144] Matthew 9:29
[145] 1 Samuel 18:1

through the deep affection that they had for each other. What we can understand from this is that a strong connection between individuals can occur to the extent of their souls become "knitted" or entwined together. When souls are connected in this way you may be acutely aware of what is happening in the soul of the other person. This connection may be good or could be damaging, especially when one person may have had traumatic experiences or has been involved with malevolent practices. The strongest soul tie occurs where there is a sexual relationship.[146] As we are aware, all of us have brokenness in our lives. Where there is a multiplicity of different sexual relationships, you become connected to a lot more brokenness, which will have a detrimental effect upon your life. That is why Scripture has a lot to say in this regard.[147]

STRONGHOLDS:

A stronghold is a fortified place in which something can hide from assault. It can also be a place from where an attack can be launched. In the spiritual realm, this may be a place in your soul, where the devil has gained some measure of control. These spiritual strongholds may also be referred to as demonic oppression[148] and in some cases demonic possession.[149]

In Ephesians we are told that there are several levels in the kingdom of Satan, each with its own sphere of domination.[150] It is these spiritual forces that can take up dominion in your soul. Let us now consider how a spiritual force can gain some sort of control over you and as a result, exert some form of power over your life.

---

[146] 1 Corinthians 6:16
[147] Act 15:29, Acts 21:25
[148] Acts 10:38
[149] Matthew 9:32
[150] Ephesians 6:12

Consider this:

I give you my credit card and I say to you that you may go and buy anything you want with my card. You go out and buy iPods, tech, furniture etc. You return home with all your purchases. Who is the owner of all those items that you bought? I paid for them and therefore have a legal right to them, but you possess them.

This is exactly what happens when you have a grievance, a hurt or hold bitterness towards people or situations. Those negative emotions and experiences are neither from God nor the fruit of the Holy Spirit, therefore they belong to Satan. Because you hold them in your heart, it is as if you have bought them on Satan's credit card. In so doing you have opened the 'door' and given the devil authority[151] by allowing wrong emotions, thoughts, feelings and fears in. You possess them and the devil has a right of access. The more you dwell on a certain negative aspects or emotions, the stronger that stronghold may become. If this continues it may migrate from demonic oppression to a demonic possession. Likewise, anything you dabble in or with that which is not of God, gives the devil access to your soul.

GENERATIONAL STRONGHOLDS:

Many times, you may experience misfortune, negative recurring events, or the effects of inappropriate behaviour despite the fact that you have tried everything to change. You may even experience demonic oppression or mental illness. Unfair as it may seem, the reason may be a result of something done or involved in by your ancestors. You may not have been involved or even been aware that such practices occurred, but they may still impact your life.[152]

---

[151] Ephesians 4:27
[152] Exodus 34:7, Deuteronomy 5:9

TACTICS, SOUL TIES & STRONGHOLDS

Let us consider what sort of practices your ancestors may have been involved with that could cause iniquity, odd responses, strange feelings and irrational behaviour in your life. These may occur:

1. If they belonged to a cult or secret society.
2. If they were involved with or practiced eastern religions, mysticism, witchcraft, transcendental meditation, sorcery, idolatry, bibliomancy,[153] Rosicrucianism, cleromancy,[154] Satanism, or necromancy.[155]
3. If they cast spells and spoke curses.
4. If they made animal or human sacrifices.
5. If they had an abortion or were involved with the practice of performing an abortion.
6. If they made ungodly covenants or were involved in or with initiation ceremonies.
7. If they had charms, idols, and occultic artefacts.
8. If they were involved in psychic healing, charming, hypnotism, magic healing, radiesthesia, pow-wow healing, power crystals or pyramid power.
9. If they practiced astral projection, levitation, mind science and mind control.
10. If they used the Ouija board, tarot cards, fortune telling, palm reading, or teacup reading to investigate or control the future.
11. If they committed adultery, failed to protect their family, or divorced.

---

[153] The use of specific words and verses for 'magical medicine'
[154] A form of divination by casting of lots or bones in which an outcome is determined or future determined
[155] The summonsing of dead people's spirits, or spirits of divination for spiritual protection, information, or wisdom

12 If they dishonoured or deceived family, friends, or business partners.

13 If they have been involved in quarrels, violence, or murders.

14 If they were involved with injustices, oppression and slavery.

15 If they had substance abuse problems, mental illnesses, gambling, squandering of resources, poverty, financial problems including bankruptcy and insolvency.

The above is not an exhaustive list but is intended to prompt you to help identify areas of possible influence. You also need to look for repeated patterns in your genealogy. It might be helpful to draw a simple family tree and add details as you get them. You should not be overwhelmed by the above list because Jesus has already freed you from the effects of your past generations. All you need to do is make it a reality in your life.

TACTICS, SOUL TIES & STRONGHOLDS

A time to look at your ancestry

Fill in the boxes with all recurring events or patterns you can think of, E.g.: Involved in occult, esoteric studies, secret societies, chronic illnesses, are deceased and the cause of death.

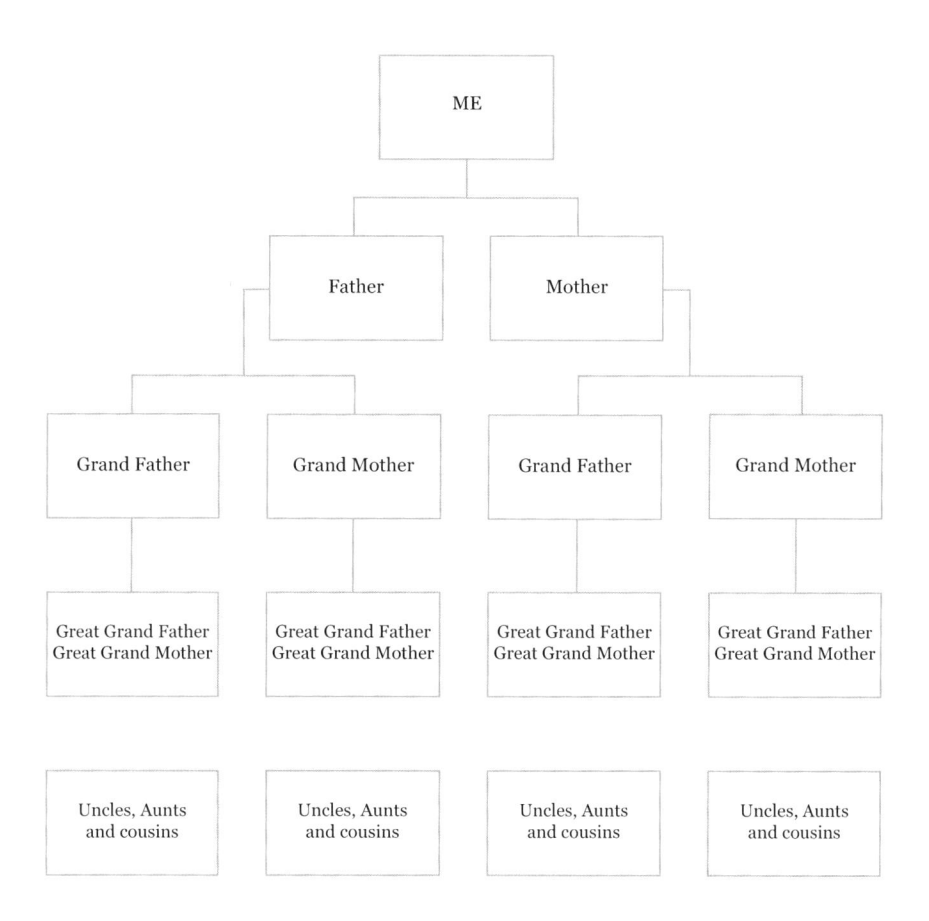

```
                            ┌──────────┐
                            │    ME    │
                            └────┬─────┘
                     ┌───────────┴───────────┐
                ┌────┴────┐             ┌────┴────┐
                │ Father  │             │ Mother  │
                └────┬────┘             └────┬────┘
           ┌────────┴────────┐      ┌───────┴────────┐
    ┌──────┴──────┐  ┌───────┴───┐ ┌─┴─────────┐  ┌──┴──────────┐
    │Grand Father │  │Grand Mother│ │Grand Father│ │Grand Mother │
    └──────┬──────┘  └───────┬───┘ └─┬─────────┘  └──┬──────────┘
           │                 │       │               │
    ┌──────┴──────┐   ┌──────┴──────┐┌┴───────────┐┌─┴───────────┐
    │Great Grand  │   │Great Grand  ││Great Grand ││Great Grand  │
    │Father       │   │Father       ││Father      ││Father       │
    │Great Grand  │   │Great Grand  ││Great Grand ││Great Grand  │
    │Mother       │   │Mother       ││Mother      ││Mother       │
    └─────────────┘   └─────────────┘└────────────┘└─────────────┘

    ┌─────────────┐   ┌─────────────┐┌────────────┐┌─────────────┐
    │Uncles, Aunts│   │Uncles, Aunts││Uncles,Aunts││Uncles, Aunts│
    │and cousins  │   │and cousins  ││and cousins ││and cousins  │
    └─────────────┘   └─────────────┘└────────────┘└─────────────┘
```

Chapter 14

THE HUMAN SPIRIT

Our human spirit is one area that most people do not have much understanding about, yet is most probably the most important part of your makeup. What is equally surprising is when it is wounded and damaged it will detrimentally impact your daily life. When your spirit is wounded, you may find that you are simply unable to get any direction or make any meaningful progress. There is a tendency to repeat the same mistake no matter how hard you try. Let us first look at how your spirit operates and helps you to live.

EXPERIENCING LIFE

Firstly, you are created to function in a similar pattern to your creator,[156] and your spirit functions in a similar manner to the Holy Spirit. The Holy Spirit gives you life[157] and it is your spirit that makes you feel alive.[158] People who have been severely wounded in their spirit, often

---

[156] Genesis 1:26-27
[157] John 3:6
[158] John 6:63, James 2:26

describe themselves as being dead inside and report that they operate only through their mind. The feeling of being alive is also experienced in worship where you experience the uplifting presence of the Lord with other believers[159]. If you have an unhealthy spirit your worship experience tends to be meaningless, and the spiritual aspect of your life is usually achieved through discipline rather than relationship.

CREATIVITY

Scripture tells us that the Holy Spirit creates[160] and in a similar manner your spirit helps you in creativity. Your healthy spirit will flow with inspiration and ideas,[161] helping you discover new ways to do things while spiritually wounded people may struggle to have new ideas.

COMMUNICATION

We communicate with the Holy Spirit through your spirit.[162] When your spirit is alive you experience God's presence and reading the Bible brings peaceful satisfaction[163]. People who have a damaged spirit may find reading the Bible difficult and also have difficulty praying. Such tasks are usually accomplished through obedience. There is also a tendency to read the same thing over and over again to try and gain comprehension.

Our spirit also helps you to connect with God 'speaking' into your heart.[164] Jesus said that you would know his 'voice'.[165] The Holy Spirit

---

[159] John 4:23-24, Psalm 46:4
[160] Genesis 2:7, Job 33:4
[161] James 1:5; 1 Corinthians 2:10
[162] I Corinthians 2:10-11
[163] Isaiah 40:31, 1Corinthians 2:14; Job 32:8
[164] Ezekiel 3:10
[165] John 10:27

also communicates with you through dreams and visions,[166] while this may be a rare experience for people with a broken spirit.

This communication connection extends to having a good conscience. Your spirit, when it is awake, warns you[167] of danger and inappropriate decisions. It can keep you out of trouble. If your spirit is asleep, you often only become aware of your wrong doing after the event[168] and to avoid getting it wrong you tend to do everything by rules and lists.

There is also a spirit-to-spirit communication with people around you. It is your spirit that gives you the ability to have a clear understanding of what others are saying or implying[169] and this communication can be so clear that you are able to perceive needs and feelings without words. The Holy Spirit communicates with you to help you intercede for others without any physical information or news about their present situation. Those struggling with a wounded spirit struggle to grasp subtle meanings and may make irrelevant comments. A broken spirit may show itself through the inability to sustain relationships or discern the needs of other.

EMPOWERMENT

The Holy Spirit strengthens[170] and empowers[171] you to accomplish many things. It is your spirit that keeps you healthy and functioning properly. You have staying power, stamina, perseverance and a lasting joy.[172] Whenever you get physically ill, your healthy spirit will help you bounce back[173] and help you recover quickly while others, with a

---

[166] Numbers 12:6-8
[167] Isaiah 30:21
[168] 1 Timothy 4:1-2
[169] 1 Corinthians 2:11-13
[170] Ephesians 3:16
[171] Acts 1:8
[172] Proverbs 17:22
[173] Proverbs 18:14

wounded spirit, may be affected by every infection going around and seem to be beset by chronic diseases.

We are further empowered here on earth by the Holy Spirit with the ability[174] to do what Jesus did[175]. You are empowered to share the Kingdom of God with others and live correctly despite the many distractions and temptations you face day by day.

ONENESS AND UNITY

There is complete harmony between the Father, the Son, and the Holy Spirit.[176] Likewise, we as believers belong to one body,[177] and unity between us[178] is achieved through our spirit being connected with God's Spirit. If your spirit is damaged, the result is disunity.

There is a special area of oneness that you can experience when a man and a woman, who are committed to each other, come together in undefiled sexual intercourse. It is more than an erotic encounter but is a coming together of spirit, soul, and body.[179] It is an intimate, precious, refreshing, creative and exhilarating experience filling the whole person. People with a wounded spirit seldom experience this complete glorifying experience but may struggle with a loss of sexual desire while romance and sex may become a duty. Wounded people may more easily fall prey to fantasy and can be more readily attracted by inappropriate opportunities.

---

[174] I Corinthians 12:8-10, 28
[175] John 14:12
[176] Genesis 1:26, John 17:11, 21-23
[177] I Corinthians 12:20
[178] Ephesians 4:3-4
[179] Genesis 2:23-24

TIMELESSNESS

In the spiritual world time does not exist as you know it and as a result there is eternity.[180] We, however, are living in a time and space continuum. With a functioning spirit we are able to move beyond the present moment and be aware of our accountability.[181] We are able draw out good things from past experiences and project them into the future, while those with a poorly functioning spirit get stuck in the present and are unable to see the pitfalls of a specific course of action.

Now that you have a better understanding of how your spirit functions, you need to understand how your spirit may have become damaged. Together, we will now examine these hindrances and blockages and the non-functioning states in which your spirit can get stuck.[182]

I am not a human being having a spiritual experience.
I am a spiritual being having a temporary human experience.

— JOHN SHEASBY —

---

[180] Hebrews 13:8
[181] Romans 14:12; Hebrews 4:12-13
[182] Recommended reading:
"Healing the Human Spirit", "Deeper Healing for the Human Spirit" by Ruth Hawkey
"Transformation of the Inner Man", "Healing the Wounded Spirit" by John and Paula Sandford

THE HUMAN SPIRIT

A time to ask a couple of questions

1   Do I enjoy worship?   yes / no
2   Do I feel the uplifting presence of the Lord
    while in a time of worship?   yes / no
3   Do I struggle to read the Bible?   yes / no
4   Do I feel that my prayers go nowhere?   yes / no
5   Do I find my time of devotions dry?   yes / no
6   Do I seldom have an original idea?   yes / no
7   Do I have to do everything by the book?   yes / no
8   Do I keep making the same mistake?   yes / no
9   Do I always misunderstand what others are saying?   yes / no
10 Do I feel fulfilled after having sex with my partner?   yes / no
11 Do I catch every germ that is going around?   yes / no
12 When I get sick, do I recover quickly?   yes / no
13 Do I have staying power and able to persevere?   yes / no
14 Am I able to empathize with people's difficulties?   yes / no

If you answered "yes" to questions 3 to 9, 11, and "no" to 1,2,10, 12 to 14 there is a strong possibility that you may have a wounded spirit.

Chapter 15

THE DYSFUNCTIONAL SPIRIT

This is not intended to be a definitive list or study but is intended so that you may begin to understand why you are struggling in one area or another. The effects of abuse and trauma will affect each of us differently and you should be careful not to jump to any conclusions but consider carefully, calling on the Holy Spirit.

A WOUNDED SPIRIT[183]

A lack of touch and nurturing in infancy and early childhood could cause a person's spirit to become stricken, broken and wounded. Continual harsh words from parents, teachers, friends, and family may leave you wounded in your spirit and in your emotions.

---

[183] Proverbs 18:14

A CRUSHED SPIRIT[184]

Your spirit can become crushed when you are forced to take on responsibilities far beyond your years. Sometimes this is forced upon you by circumstances and sometimes by overbearing manipulation and control of people in authority over you. If you have a crushed spirit, you may have a severe lack of self-worth, struggle with self-pity and have a deep sadness to the point of wanting to give up on life. If you have a crushed spirit, you may continually be seeking or need affirmation.

A SLUMBERING SPIRIT[185]

Here your spirit is unable to receive correct information either through the soul or the Holy Spirit. The result is that you are unable to hear or grasp information. Your intuition, creativity and communication are impaired. This may have been a traumatic experience where you were shocked into numbness. Involvement in the occult or generational strongholds may also be a factor.

A BROKEN SPIRIT[186]

Your spirit may be broken when you suffered an intense loss, perhaps by the loss of a parent at a very crucial stage of development. Traumas experienced at birth and while still in the womb (including unsuccessful abortions) can also break your spirit. In later life rejection, betrayal, and any form of abuse could cause damage. If you have a broken spirit, you may experience illnesses, deep sadness, sorrow, inability to trust, premature aging and often have trouble sleeping, sometimes only falling asleep just when you need to get up.

---

[184] Psalm 143:3, Isaiah 61:3
[185] Romans 11:8
[186] Job 17:1, Proverbs 15:13, 17:22

A TIMID SPIRIT[187]

Timidity and fearfulness can be caused by a trauma in childhood or through generational strongholds. When these become severe, your spirit is also impacted. When you struggle with this type of damage, you may carry an anxiety about life that is more than just emotional. You can be guarded in your relationships but are constantly in need of love and assurance. You usually fear the worst of every situation or relationship.

A DEFILED SPIRIT[188]

Here your spirit is contaminated and spiritually dirty. This could happen through ungodly soul ties, generational strongholds, idolatry or having partaken in the occult, be it

willingly or unwillingly. When you are contaminated, you may find it difficult to worship, or confess and forgive. You may be confused and have little control over the words you speak.[189] Blasphemy and swearing are also indicators of defilement.[190]

AN IMPRISONED SPIRIT[191]

With an imprisoned spirit your spirit is chained and bound. It is like being in a dungeon away from your body and soul. If you are struggling with an imprisoned spirit, you may describe yourself as feeling dead or empty inside. It is something like walking into a big empty hall with nothing inside or nobody at home. You may often feel you are living in a glass box. You may be able to see and perceive but often feel isolated.

---

[187] 2 Timothy 1:7
[188] 2 Corinthians 7:1
[189] James 3:5,6,8
[190] James 3:9-10
[191] Psalm 142:7, 143:3, Isaiah 42:20-22

THE DYSFUNCTIONAL SPIRIT

Your world may often feel cold, and you may seem unable to enjoy the subtleties and the rich textures that make life enjoyable[192]. Such a dramatic condition may be caused through torture, enforced isolation, enforced starvation, domination, and emotional or mind control. If you as a child or an adult have been subjected to continued ritual and sexual abuse, severe spiritual damage has been caused, which can result in an impaired and distorted view of life with complicated behavioural patterns. The recovery process may often take a long time.

Despite the events that life may throw at you, your God is still bigger than them all and with Him nothing is impossible.[193] In the next chapter you will look at spiritual restoration.

We can become so comfortable with our pain that we become unwilling to step out in faith and embrace all that Jesus has purchased for us.

— MARGIE (MY WIFE) —

---

[192] Author's note: I am not describing autism or people with neural diversity although the experiences are very similar.
[193] Luke 1:37

A ROAD TO FREEDOM

A time to take stock

1	Was I continually subjected to harsh words?	yes / no
2	Did I take on responsibility beyond my years?	yes / no
3	Was I subjected to manipulation and control?	yes / no
4	Did I experience a shock that left me feeling numb?	yes / no
5	Did I experience continual rejection as a child?	yes / no
6	Was I abused emotionally, physically or sexually?	yes / no
7	Was I forced to take part in something ugly?	yes / no
8	Did I attend meetings that made me feel uneasy?	yes / no
9	Do I feel dead inside?	yes / no
10	Was I bullied, threatened, or tortured?	yes / no
11	Was I continually taunted or teased?	yes / no
12	Am I adopted or fostered?	yes / no
13	Was I forced to take part in any occultic rituals?	yes / no

Please remember, if you answered, "yes" to any of the above questions, it was not your fault and you did not deserve to be treated that way but, there is a possibility that you may have a damaged spirit.

Chapter 16

SPIRITUAL RESTORATION

Spiritual restoration is most effectively achieved through prayer and by inviting the Holy Spirit to minister to you, for without Him you can do nothing.[194] Your starting point is always to notice those things in your behaviour and your responses that are causing you problems and are not reflecting the fruit of the Holy Spirit. Once you know what you need to deal with, you will need to confess, forgive, and cancel any resentment you may have towards people. Now you are ready to tackle the spiritual side.

Here are a few guidelines that you need to follow when dealing with spiritual issues. Firstly, you need to establish your authority[195] in Jesus, as this will restrict the demonic spirits[196] and avoid unnecessary struggles or manifestations. This is usually covered at the beginning when we pray. The sample prayers in Appendix 2 always begin with the establishment of your spiritual authority.

---

[194] Romans 11:36
[195] Luke 9:1, 10:19
[196] Matthew 12:29

You will then need to deal with the specific spiritual issue/s through prayer, and preferably with someone[197]. After dealing with the issue, you will need seal any access used by Satan, with the blood[198] of Jesus. After that you will need to invite the Holy Spirit to refresh you and fill[199] the vacated areas[200] of your soul with love, joy, peace, etc.[201] Finally, you need to give thanks, honour, and glory to your Heavenly Father. It is through Jesus' sacrifice for our indiscretions,[202] that we are cleansed and are protected.

It is recommended that you seek the assistance of someone who has an understanding and experience in spiritual restoration when dealing with strongholds and especially when your spirit has been wounded. I have included some sample prayers as guidelines in the appendix. The prayers cover the aspects as discussed above.

It is strongly suggested that all prayers should be prayed aloud.

GENERATIONAL STRONGHOLDS

Again, when dealing with generational strongholds it is strongly recommended that there be another person present, as you may not know what may surface. Usually there are a combination of issues that need to be considered, your own ancestral iniquity, ungodly soul ties, spiritual forces, cancelling of curses and repenting on behalf of your ancestors. I suggest you should identify the practice and/or event you are dealing with – for example, like Tarot card reading. It is not necessary to understand that practice to be able to deal with it, so please don't go researching it before hand on the internet. This will only make matters worse.

---

[197] Matthew 18:19
[198] Exodus 12:23
[199] Ephesians 5:18
[200] Matthew 12:43-45
[201] Galatians 5:22,23
[202] Hebrews 10:10

I would suggest that you should begin by dealing with your own ancestral iniquity[203] [204].

It may also be necessary, to stand in the gap for your previous generations[205], asking forgiveness on their behalf, for the Father to forgive them for their part in the iniquity. If prompted by the Holy Spirit, you can ask forgiveness from those who were hurt. Although you may not know who they are, you could pray saying, "Father, in the name of Jesus, you ask that those hurt by the actions of my ancestors, that they would forgive my ancestors and me for any wrong done by us to them."

CURSES

Next, we should consider all curses spoken by yourself and those spoken over you by others. When dealing with any curses, incantations, initiations, oaths, or pledges and any destructive or harmful words, you should first confess these as sin. You need to ask the Lord for forgiveness for speaking that way. It is useful to speak forgiveness towards those that spoke negative words over you and your life. It is beautiful to ask the Lord to reverse the curse[206] and turn it into a blessing and thank Him for doing so.[207]

SOUL TIES

Here we are dealing with ungodly soul ties, not the Godly ties which you may have, as example, with a parent. What is important is that you do not judge, but honour the person by, firstly not blaming them for your problems. You honour them when you acknowledge that they, like you, did not fully comprehend the implications of their actions. The most important soul ties are those created through any sexual

---

[203] Leviticus 26:40-42, Nehemiah 9:2
[204] See appendix 2 for prayer: Ancestral Iniquity
[205] See appendix 2 for prayer: Intercession on behalf of my previous generations
[206] Deuteronomy 23:5
[207] See Appendix 2 for Cancellation of Curses prayer.

activities,[208] irrespective if it was physically or any other activity. If there have been a number of different sexual contacts, you may not be able to remember all the names. This is not critical, rather you pray saying, "I forgive that one" and later, "I break every ungodly soul tie with that one." If you can remember their names, you should mention them individually. Do not let it trouble you if you cannot remember all their names, but understand, the Lord knows everything. You need to acknowledge them. It is He who makes you clean and restores you.[209]

STRONGHOLDS

When dealing with spiritual strongholds, I strongly recommend, you do this with someone who is experienced in this area.

Demonic forces gain access to your soul when you partake in any ungodly practices or harbour negative emotions. If you try to get rid of the demonic spirit before you have removed their right of access,[210] you will have a fight on your hands. You first need to deal with any resentment, negative emotions or ungodly practices that has given the demonic access before you can tell that demonic spirit to leave.

Here is a useful illustration:

There is a rather unpleasant person squatting in a house in the neighbourhood. Because he is causing a lot of trouble, I decide I need to get rid of him and take over the house. With the help of a couple of my friends, we forcibly throw him out of the house. He tries to resist but we overpower him. I now take possession of the house but because he is use to living there, he keeps looking for a way to get back inside. The moment I am off guard, he is inside. He might even get some of his friends to help him.[211] But let us assume that I have now gained legal right to the house by purchasing

---

[208] 1 Corinthian 6:16
[209] See Appendix 2 for a Soul Ties prayer.
[210] Mark 3:27
[211] Luke 11:24-26

SPIRITUAL RESTORATION

the house. When I come to take possession, I find that he is still there and refusing to move. Because I now have a legal right, I no longer need to fight him but can simply have him evicted by the authorities.

There are only a limited number of types of demonic spirits[212] recorded in the Bible. When I am casting out an oppressive demonic spirit, I address each spirit type with a firm but calm voice. I don't need to shout but simply command, for example, "Spirit of lies, I command you in the name of Jesus to leave (*name*) now." I will then get the person to repeat my words while I watch what is happening in them. I will then deal with the next spirit type. There is a list of the different spirit types with their characteristics in the appendix.[213] When dealing with this form of restoration, I always keep eye contact with the person I am praying for so that I can observe what is happening.

I have included two different prayers for spiritual strongholds[214]. The first is if you yourself have **not** been involved in the occult and/or esoteric practices. The second prayer is if you have personally been involved in the occult and/or esoteric practices

RESTORATION OF THE DAMAGED SPIRIT

Damage to your spirit is caused by broken relationships. You were never created to live in isolation[215] and we all need human contact, love, nurturing and acceptance. If at any stage of your development, this relationship process is broken, you will suffer physically, emotionally, and spiritually.[216] If you have worked through your emotional healing process, many of the things that caused damage to your spirit may have already been addressed and the healing of your spirit would have

---

[212] Recommended reading "By their fruits you shall know them" by Mary Garrison
[213] See Appendix 4.
[214] See Appendix 2 for Spiritual Stronghold prayers.
[215] John 15:6
[216] Recommended reading "Changes that Heal" by Dr. Henry Cloud

already begun, but there are a few additional things you may need to look at.

If you have a damaged spirit, you will need people around you, who you can share your brokenness with[217], without fear of judgment and recrimination. You need people around you who will "walk" with you at your own pace,[218] where you can discover who you are and come to know the unconditional love of your Heavenly Father.[219] It is the Holy Spirit who restores your spirit, and this is often accomplished through the laying on of hands[220] in prayer.[221]

Often, you may be a little impatient and may think that once you have dealt with one type of situation, that all such similar situations are dealt with. Unfortunately, this is not always the case. You may need to repeat the process for each situation[222] and any events as the Holy Spirit brings it to mind.[223] It may seem a long road, but actually it is not, because it just gets better and better. God has not given up on you. What He has started He has promised to finish.[224]

People often look to books, podcasts, programs, courses, CD's or people to solve their problems. The only way your problems are completely solved is through the Lord changing your heart and destroying your bondages.

— MERRIL —

---

[217] Galatians 6:2
[218] Genesis 33:13-14
[219] Jeremiah 31:3
[220] 2 Timothy 1:6-7
[221] See Appendix 2 for prayer Healing for the wounded spirit
[222] Matthew 12:36
[223] John 14:26
[224] Philippians 1:6

SPIRITUAL RESTORATION

A time to decide

Do you think that there may be some ungodly soul ties that need to be dealt with? List them if you feel comfortable.

_____

_____

_____

_____

Do you think that there may be some spiritual strongholds that need to be dealt with? List them, if you are able to.

_____

_____

_____

_____

Do you think that there may be some generational strongholds that need to be dealt with?

_____

_____

_____

_____

Part 3

PHYSICAL RESTORATION

Chapter 17

HEALING BODY MEMORIES

As mentioned in the beginning of this book, you are a spirit, soul, and body. So far, we have discussed the spirit and the soul. Now it is time to look at how the body and the brain function.

What happens in your spirit and soul is reflected in the body. You usually take note that something is wrong when your body is feeling unwell. What you see, feel, and experience creates thoughts[225], which in turn form neural pathways[226] in the brain. These neural pathways, if negative, will cause the body to breakdown as described in Chapter 11. An amazing aspect of the body is that God created the body to heal itself and if you start improving your thought life, the body starts to heal.

EXPLICIT AND IMPLICIT MEMORIES

Our upper brain is divided into left and right hemispheres. The left side has to do with sequencing and processing while the right with

---

[225] Mathew 6:23
[226] Neural pathway: a series of connected neurons that send signals from one part of the brain to another; www.greatmindsclinic.co.uk

1.
2.
3.
4.
5.
6.
7.
8.
9.
10.
11.
12.
13.
14.
15.
16.
17.
18.
19.
20.

emotional processing. In the left side of the brain is a speech center called the Broca. The left side of the brain only starts to become active from about age two and a half.

Before age two and a half, the child is processing information in the right side of the brain. This accounts for why very few have recallable memories before age 3. Recallable memories are referred to as explicit memories which only occur when the Broca can process the speech and language functions.

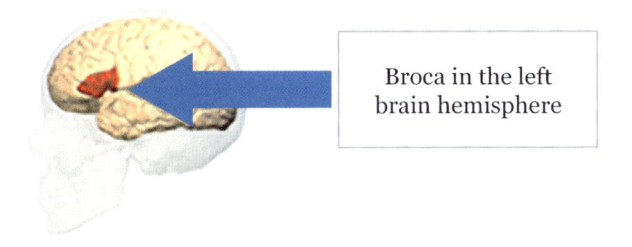

Broca in the left brain hemisphere

Source: en.wikipedia.org/wiki/Broca%27s_area

But you also have memories without words. These are implicit memories and are stored in the lower brain and the body. A good example of this is when you are driving your car, you are not aware how your feet are moving and pressing the various pedals. This is done implicitly, but you may remember the first time you got into a car to learn to drive. This is called an explicit memory.

Implicit memories can be recognized by feelings in the body, emotions, and responding thoughts. An example of this is a person who may have had a forceps delivery at birth. They will often feel uncomfortable if someone touches their head, often with strong emotional reaction. All of this is triggered and activated by the lower brain.

THE TRIUNE BRAIN

The human brain is complex but some simple ideas about its function are helpful. There are upper and lower parts to the brain. The upper brain or neocortex is responsible for higher-order brain functions like your 5 senses, the choices you may make, your thoughts, emotional understanding, and speech. Your lower or back brain has subconscious and unconscious functions, and consisting of two main parts, your reptilian brain and limbic (mammalian) brain. The reptilian brain keeps your vital functions, like heart and lungs, operating while the mammalian brain has more to do with subconscious memories and experiences. Within the lower brain is the amygdala, which is much like a smoke alarm. The amygdala functions to keep you safe from any threats. Input from the 5 physical senses is filtered and then passed on to the lower and the upper brains. The amygdala reads the sensory information, and if this information is deemed as dangerous, it activates an instinctive respond within 7 milliseconds, irrespective if the danger is real or not.

For example, if a ball was thrown at you randomly, you respond 'automatically' by ducking or blocking. You become aware of this 'automatic' response only after the event. Usually there is an increase in heart rate, faster breathing; sometimes you may experience tension, fear, anxiety, shock, or numbness. When this instinctive response system is activated, blood is drawn away from the upper brain which can hinder your ability to think logically or speak clearly. In extreme situations you may experience amnesia even though you can continue to engage with events around you. If a threat is regularly perpetrated, as in repeated child abuse, dissociation[227] may occur. Later you may have no or very little recall of what happened. Whenever threatened, there is a need to find safety, comfort, and release. Satisfying the need for comfort can form addictive behaviour patterns due to your dopamine receptors being stimulated and a resultant release of DeltaFosB, resulting in an urge of wanting to do it again.

---

[227] Dissociation is the disconnection from a current reality to avoid pain

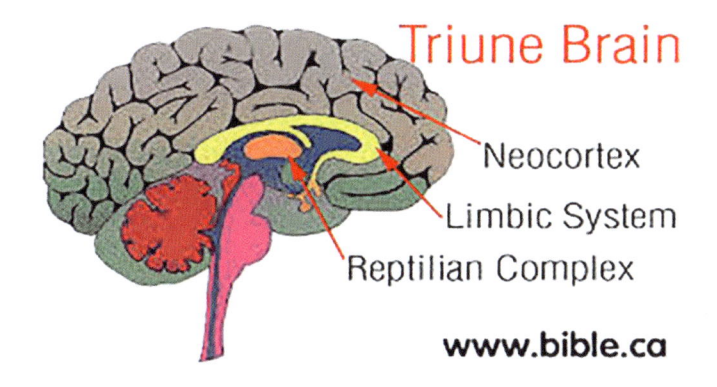

SOMATIC MEMORIES[228]

As we discuss somatic memory, please be aware that not all somatic memory is bad or unhelpful. Somatic memory is vital for everyday functions like walking or driving a car. But often, you experience reactions that are unhelpful in living life effectively. An example may be a fear of spiders, or loud noises. Sometimes it is a fear of relationships or social situations. Often these are caused by trauma which may also result in dissociation. Despite your best efforts, there is an overreaction. You may find that all the efforts to renew the mind, repentance, praying, learning scripture, does not changing that behavior, often resulting in frustration and hopelessness. It can often lead to low moods or depression. These implicit memories need to be dealt with differently.

Our brain has been designed to resolve mild invasive events like a minor motorcar accident. This resolution may take a time, from days to months. Unfortunately, there are times when your brain is unable to resolve the experience and you become stuck, which may result in unhelpful behavior patterns. There are several different treatments, and it is suggested that this work should be done in consultation with a suitably trained and experienced practitioner.

---

[228] Somatic memories and memories stored in the nervous system of the body resulting from previous experiences and learning.

There are three suggested treatments that would be useful to explore. There is Sensorimotor Psychotherapy, Emotional Freedom Technique (EFT) and Eye Movement Desensitization and Reprocessing (EMDR). These techniques work with the memory held in the body and in the lower brain while maintaining an understanding that in the present you are safe and there is no danger.

Finally, I have found that in my experience, that these techniques are very effective but full resolution is only ultimately achieved when combined with all the other suggestions previously described in this book.

Chapter 18

GOD'S VIEW ON PHYSICAL HEALING

When it comes to the subject of physical healing, there is a lot of confusion especially for those that understand we have healing through the New Covenant. The result is that often we may adopt a way of thinking to explain why we are not healed.

The Father's heart, from the beginning of time, is that you should be healthy and prosper. His first instructions were that you should be productive, successful, and increase abundantly[229] which you cannot do when you are sick. When you do become sick, God has said that He will cure you.[230] God is unchanging[231] and when Jesus was living here on earth, he did not come only die for your sins, but also to reveal the Father[232] to you. Throughout the whole Bible, the Father's heart, of restoration in every area of life, is revealed. Jesus said that he and

---

[229] Genesis 1:22
[230] Jeremiah 30:17, Psalm 103:3
[231] Hebrews 13:8,
[232] John 14:8-9

the Father are one.[233] Wherever Jesus went he did good, provided for, cared for and healed people[234], demonstrating the heart of your Father. The only people who didn't get better were those who didn't believe.[235] The beginning point for your healing is that you need to believe you can get well.

Not only did the Father demonstrate healing through Jesus, but you also have marvellous accounts of how Peter, John and many others demonstrated the Father's intention that you should be healthy.[236] Today, all over the world there are many healing miracles taking place, again confirming the Father's intention to bring wholeness to your body.

When Satan can get you to believe that physical healing is not yours, he will then try to get you think that it is God who made you sick. Unless you know and are convinced that the Father wants you healthy, you will accept your condition and stop seeking Him for healing.

---

[233] John 10:30
[234] Matthew 4:24, 8:16, Mark 1:34, Luke 4:18,40
[235] Matthew 13:58
[236] Acts 3:4-8

A time to review

What is your view on physical healing?

_____

_____

_____

_____

Do you believe there is healing for you?

_____

_____

_____

_____

What do you think you need to do to receive physical healing?

_____

_____

_____

_____

Chapter 19

WHY ARE ONLY SOME HEALED?

This is a difficult question to answer. What I share here is my understanding[237] but I firmly believe God can heal, and wants you to be healed, even if you are not healed.

What we have got to keep in mind, there is God's part and the part that you play in the healing process. You have been given a free will and while here on earth, the Father will not force you to do anything. The choice you make is yours and yours alone. Imagine you want to jump off a bridge into a river. The Holy Spirit will warn you that it is not safe, but the choice to jump or listen is yours. You need to choose. Even believing that God can heal you is a choice.

When it comes to your negative and destructive thinking patterns, it is your responsibility to choose to think differently[238]. You must choose to think differently[239].

---

[237] 1 Corinthian 13:12
[238] 2 Corinthian 10:5
[239] Romans 12:2

This same concept is also applicable to the subconscious and unconscious thoughts that are generated from our lower brain as discussed in Chapter 17. That is the reason why EFT and EMDR technique are so effective. These techniques help you to be renewed in your subconscious and unconscious minds and leave past experiences in the past and believe something differently now.

When it comes to healing you must not try to do God's part. Your part is to acknowledge and take responsibility for any negative emotions and negative words. Your part is to renew your mind, which you can do with the help of Holy Spirit. Your part is to go to the Heavenly Father and surrender[240].

Because we are human, as we get older parts of our body wear out. This is a natural progression of all life. Secondly, there are viruses, bacteria, poisons, and forms of contamination – all of these will have a detrimental effect upon your body. With a healthy spirit you can age with dignity and recover from sickness. All these normal effects are exacerbated when you abuse your bodies through strenuous activities beyond which the body was designed for and by an unhealthy lifestyle. The increase of refined foods laden with preservatives does not help too much either.

I believe it is our thought life that is the main contributor to ill health and not getting healed. I believe that when we approach the Father, we need to have the correct attitude and respect. I believe that if your motivation for what you are seeking the Heavenly Father for is rooted in your own ego and not based in surrender[241], the Father cannot fulfill what He wants to, which is to restore and bless you. Your Heavenly Father cannot heal you on your terms, for then, you would approach Him for everything in a similar manner. It must be in the manner He has established.

---

[240] Matthew 16:25
[241] Matthew 16:24-26

As a result of trauma and hurt that you have experienced, you may have developed a negative psychological way of thinking that contributes enormously to your physical breakdown. Your body is the reflector of the condition of your spirit and soul[242] and as you seek your emotional and spiritual healing your body will respond by becoming healthier.

Pastor Henry Wright has done some excellent work, listing the psychosomatic roots of diseases.[243] For example, cancer could be the result of bitterness. Bitterness causes dysfunction of the immune system, which causes the deterioration of proto-oncogenes. When proto-oncogenes are missing, the body cells are compromised allowing oncogenes to turn healthy cells into cancerous cells. Exposure to atomic radiation can also kill anti-oncogenes that will then result in tumors and growths. This research has been further supported by the work of Dr M K Strydom.[244]

Medical research today further confirms that your physical health is dependent upon the state of your emotional and psychological well-being. Psychosomatic illnesses are well researched and further research in the field of cardiology has now shown that your emotional state will greatly affect your heart whether you suffer from heart disease or not. Other research has shown that your blood composition changes when you harbor bitterness.[245] There are many drugs and treatments that can reverse the effects of endocrine and psychological dysfunction, but they might not be dealing with the primary cause.

My personal viewpoint is that dealing with the symptoms does not deal with the real cause. Alternatively, by altering a dysfunctional behaviour and not addressing the primary cause, the problem may reoccur in another form. If you can tackle the problem at the source, then a

---

[242] Proverbs 4:23, 14:30, 15:13, 15:15, 17:22, 18:14
[243] "A More Excellent Way" by Pastor Henry Wright
[244] Healing Begins with the Sanctification of the Heart 'No Disease is Incurable' - Dr MK Strydom, Second Edition 2010
[245] "Changes that Heal" by Dr. Henry Cloud

WHY ARE ONLY SOME HEALED?

whole host of problems can be resolved. Added to that, any applied interventions are then more effective.

Faith, or the lack of it, may also contribute to you not being healed. Healing seldom occurs if you are unable to believe[246] in your heart[247] (not your head) that God can heal you. Alternatively, you may believe that God can heal but are unwillingly to admit[248] you have wrong attitudes or may be unprepared to be changed. While you are not surrendering, you are immature[249] and your healing will be delayed.

It is a sad moment when you have taken the courage to be prayed for, to be told it is because you lack faith that you are not healed. The fact that you went there in the first place is an act of faith. Hopefully when faced with such harsh words, you will not give up but continue to go to the Lord and ask what you need to change to receive your healing.

Lastly, and I believe this is an important factor; the Lord wants you to mature.[250] You may often seek healing but are unwilling to examine your attitudes. You may hold grudges but be unwilling to forgive. You may be worried but are unable to trust. You may be more concerned about your own importance rather than having regard for others. You may want others to overlook your own shortcomings but are unable to tolerate the shortcomings of others. These attitudes indicate that there is still a maturing process that needs to happen.

If you could be miraculously healed every time you became sick, you would not learn to take care of your bodies and ultimately, you would be no better than a spoilt child that throws a tantrum whenever it cannot get what it wants.

---

[246] Mark 6:5-6
[247] Author's note: I believe the heart in the Bible refers to our unconscious and sub-conscious processing of the lower brain and negative somatic memories
[248] James 5:16
[249] Colossians 1:28, Hebrews 6:1
[250] 1 Corinthians 14:20

The purpose of this book is simply to help you confront your fears, your attitudes, your weaknesses, and your places of brokenness with the realisation that you cannot change without the help of the Lord. What is exciting is that you can go to the Lord in full confidence,[251] without fear or shame. Nobody can do this for you. This is your personal journey, although people may be able to help you, encourage you, and strengthen you in your struggle.[252] Having someone to walk with you is important and useful but you still have to do it.

Our Heavenly Father seeks a relationship not a religious practice. Religion, by definition, is a system of moral and ethical practices which man adopts to make himself right with his god through his own effort.

— MERRIL —

---

[251] Hebrews 4:16
[252] 1 Thessalonians 5:14 - 15

WHY ARE ONLY SOME HEALED?

A time to examine

What aspects of your lifestyle do you need to change so that you can be healthier?

_____
_____
_____
_____

What attitudes do you think you may need to change that can improve your health?

_____
_____
_____
_____

What do you think you can do to increase your faith for physical healing?

_____
_____
_____
_____

Chapter 20

RESTORATION AND SELF CARE

As you read this section of the book, it will be helpful for you to understand my meaning of the word's "illness" and "disease"[253]. Both result in sickness. I use the word "disease" in the meaning of any external pathogen that can infect your body. "Illness" is used in the context of a breakdown of personal heath resulting from negative thoughts and emotions. I am very aware, that people struggling with acute depression may find that some of the following suggestions difficult to implement. But may I encourage you, to give it a try, even if it is a very small step[254].

Often, you may live in denial of the fact that you have a problem that may be manifesting itself in a physical illness. Sometimes it is only when you admit and accept, you have a problem, can healing begin to happen. You may need to give up the idea that you can "fix it". This acceptance of your own personal helplessness initiates submission[255] and surrender. Until that point, you have a form of pride.[256]

---

[253] Psalm 103:3-4
[254] I have included a prayer for praying in Difficult Situation – see Appendix 2
[255] Ephesians 5:21
[256] Leviticus 26:19, Proverbs 11:2, 29:23

RESTORATION AND SELF CARE

When you are sick or ill, you need to see a medical practitioner. Once a professional diagnosis has been made, you can begin to consider if there are emotional and spiritual components. If there are, then you may tackle these simultaneously. If medical interventions make it difficult to embark upon this phase, you can either work slowly or put it on hold for a while. On no account is it recommended that you stop taking any prescribed medication without consulting your physician.

We also need to ensure you are getting enough sleep[257] and eating healthily. This may be particularly difficult if you have problems with sleeping or are struggling with an eating disorder. Again, you may put this on hold until you are stronger and then embark on any number of interventions that will help you break the destructive cycle.

There is another factor that needs to be considered and may often be overlooked. Heavy metal toxicity occurs when you have been exposed to chemicals such as copper, mercury, lead, cadmium, aluminium, or arsenic. These chemicals can often be passed down through the placenta of the mother in the womb. Heavy metals may cause tremors, headaches, infertility, anxiety, and depression. They may also affect memory, eyes, kidneys, the digestive system, and your immune function. Another side effect can be tingling in the extremities and around your mouth[258] area.

In 2007, The World Health Organisation put out the following statement regarding Heavy Metal Toxicity; *"…are associated to different degrees with a wide range of conditions, including kidney and bone damage, developmental and neuro-behavioural disorders, elevated blood pressure, and potentially even lung cancer."*

Fortunately, today, such toxicity can be treated by a qualified health professional. This may be done using substances that bind to the heavy

---

[257] Suggested reading: Brainstorm by Dr Daniel Siegel, Mindsight Practice B: Sleep Time
[258] https://www.thorne.com/take-5-daily/article/the-impacts-of-heavy-metal-toxicity

metals to facilitate removal from the body. It is recommended that such treatment should be carried out under the guidance of a suitably qualified health professional who would first test for the toxicity and be able to target the specific heavy metal.

We need to get regular and appropriate exercise. To begin with you may think of starting with rebounding exercises[259] especially if you have been sick for a long time. This is particularly good to get the lymphatic system functioning again.

When you are sick, you are more aware of your own misery than what is around you. This may tend to isolate you. Wherever possible you need to have contact and create friendships with other people.[260] These friendships help you to give and receive love. When you love others,[261] your concern for their well-being becomes more important than your own discomfort. This change of attitude aids your healing.[262]

It is important to try and have some fun. Laughter is very therapeutic,[263] helping your bodies to recover by reducing blood pressure, stress levels, boosting your immunity[264] and producing endorphins, which are natural pain relievers.[265] You can have fun and laugh by reading an amusing book, watching comedy or the antics of animals and reminiscing over happy moments with friends and family.

If you dwell on the negatives, the negativity will overwhelm you. The reverse is equally true. For you to be healthy you need a positive frame of mind.[266] A good way to achieve this is by reading stories of what

---

[259] http://www.healingdaily.com/exercise/rebounding-for-detoxification-and-health.htm
[260] Genesis 2:18
[261] John 15:13
[262] Isaiah 58:10
[263] Proverbs 15:13
[264] http://www.naturalnews.com/026311.html
[265] http://en.wikipedia.org/wiki/Endorphin
[266] Philippians 4:8

God can do through the lives of people like John G Lake, Katherine Kuhlmann and many, many others.[267]

Listening to talks that "don't beat you up" and inspirational speakers like John and Bev Sheasby,[268] who understand God's goodness and grace can help you change the way you view things. Likewise, listening to inspirational music will help you to have a better frame of mind, which in turn will help the body recover.

Attending conferences where there is a strong presence of the Holy Spirit is recommended. It is often in these types of conferences, as you surrender yourselves to God the Holy Spirit, that many miraculous healings can take place.

Thankfulness and gratitude have a significant impact on your health and well-being[269]. May I suggest having a thankfulness journal. Write down everything you can be thankful for, like having a bed, clothes, food, that you may be able to function physically. Also, at the end of the day, write down everything thing you can think of that you can be thankful for, like the bus arriving when you went out. When you are feeling down, take out your journal and remind yourself what you can be thankful for. Thankfulness opens your connection with the Heavenly Father[270].

Lastly, and this is vital. Learn to live in the present moment. When you are aware of what is happening in the present moment, you will be able to notice changes in your body, like your heart beating faster because of fear. You will be able to notice your emotions. You will be able to notice your thoughts and stop them spiraling into negativity[271]. If you are not living and being aware in the present moment, then you will be unable to achieve much as you will be unable to

---

[267] Hebrews 12:1
[268] http://www.liberatedliving.com/media.html
[269] The 28 benefits of gratitude - https://positivepsychology.com
[270] Psalm 100:4
[271] 2 Corinthians 10:5

hear the voice of the Holy Spirit. When you are living in the past and dwelling on regrets, Jesus cannot help you, as He isn't there. He was there when it happened. If you are anxious and fearful, you are living in the future and Jesus is not there either. He will be there when you get to that point in the future. Jesus is in your present moment, so if you want to live by the spirit, you need to be living in the present moment.

And finally, you need to persevere.[272]

Our Personal Testimonies:

I was an asthmatic from age 3. All my life I have sought healing and around age 40 I had given up any hope that I could be healed from asthma. At that time, I could not live without daily medication. A little while after that I came to know the Lord and learnt that God can heal. It took another 15 years before I was completely healed. Today, I am totally free from asthma. Much of what I learnt about healing and restoration in those 15 years has been recorded in this book.

My wife struggled with bi-polar disorder (manic depression). She tried to commit suicide on two occasions. After she came to know the Lord, she learnt there was healing. It took her 5 years to become completely healed. Today, those dark days are just a memory.

Sometimes healing is quick, sometimes it may take a long time, but you must not lose hope for God does heal!

> *Faith is the opposite of fear.*
> *Both are based on what we believe.*
>
> — MERRIL —

This is not the end ......**This is the beginning!**

---

[272] 2 Peter 1:5-7

RESTORATION AND SELF CARE

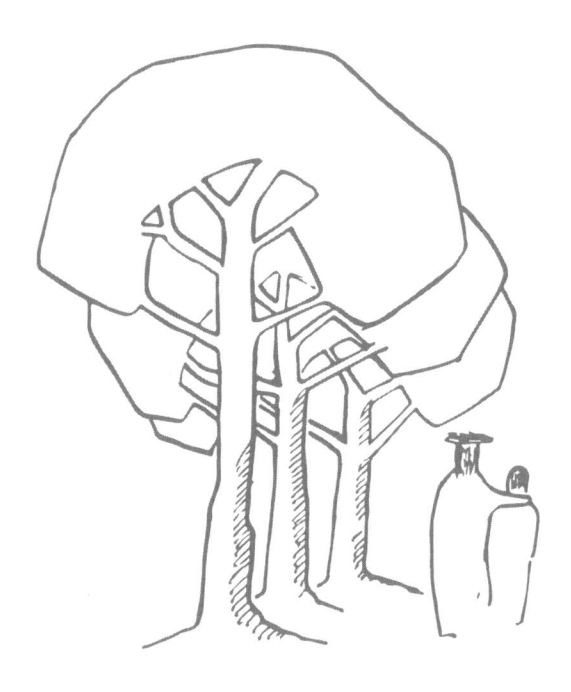

A ROAD TO FREEDOM

A time for action

1. In your private journal, write down the issues, attitudes, behaviours or struggles in your life at this moment that you want to change.

2. Choose one of the above that you feel the Holy Spirit wants you to deal with.

3. Decide on the steps that you are going to implement. Write them down in your journal.

4. Using your diary, set a date when you are going to implement those steps.

5. Review your progress after you have implemented each step.

6. After one week, review how much restoration has taken place.

7. Diarise a date approximately one month later to review how much restoration has now occurred.

8. Once you are satisfied with the restoration that has taken place, with the help of the Holy Spirit, choose the next issue.

9. If you are not satisfied that sufficient restoration has occurred, review step 3 above and implement steps 4 to 6.

10. If you are still not satisfied that sufficient restoration has occurred then decide whom you can talk to about your problem. Make contact with them by whichever means you feel is appropriate.

Part 3

APPENDICES

Appendix 1

CASE STUDY

In 1999, I was washing the dishes for my wife. She wanted to make me some coffee and came to the sink to draw water. I had to stand aside while she drew water from the tap. As I stood to the side, with my hands still over the sink, I started feeling irritated and a thought ran through my mind: "You are in my way!" Margie discerned that I was irritated. She asked, "What's the matter?" I growled back, "Nothing's wrong!" Margie, in her wisdom, left me to cool down.

I asked myself the question "Was this irritation displaying the fruit of the Holy Spirit? Was it peace? No! Was it love? No! Was it joy? No, absolutely not! Was it patience, gentleness, kindness, goodness, patience, or self-control?" This irritation that I experienced was not the fruit of the Holy Spirit and therefore I didn't want it because it was unpleasant.

Next morning, I said to the Lord, "Father, I've got a problem!" He answered me, "Yes, I know." "Lord, my reaction yesterday was not pleasing to you, and I don't want to react like that again. I know it is the result[273] of an unresolved issue in my heart. Lord, what is that unresolved issue that I may bring it before Your Throne of Grace so that you can change me?"

I then sat quietly reflecting on the Lord with some gentle music in the background. I prayed, "Holy Spirit please show me the root cause." Within minutes a memory popped into my head. If nothing had happened, I

---

[273] Matthew 7:16

would have put it on hold because I knew the Holy Spirit would show me something in a day or two. The answer could also have been revealed to me through a dream or a prophetic word from another person.

This is what I remembered. I must have been about 3 or 4 years old. I wanted to do a job for my mother, but I also had my own agenda. My mother always kept a packet of sweets in the cupboard, and I had been told, "If you are a good boy, you can have a sweet." My reasoning was that if I helped her, I would be a good boy and would get a sweet. There I was, working away, doing the job to the best of my ability. Along comes my mother and says, "You're in my way!" It was exactly the same words that had popped into my mind while I was washing the dishes for my wife. When my mother had said those words, I had become upset, because I thought it meant that I was not a good boy and therefore I would not get my sweet.

Now that the root of my problem had been revealed, I began by confessing that I had this problem of being irritated when someone gets in my way. I asked the Lord to forgive me for my bad behaviour towards my mother and my wife.

I also needed to forgive my mother. All I knew was that I had these negative feelings, and I was struggling because of them. I was doing a job for my mother, but she was annoyed with me for no apparent reason. All I could perceive was that there was no reward, and I was unable to forgive from my heart. I had to get inside my mother's 'shoes' to understand what caused her to respond that way. I needed help so I said, "Holy Spirit, please put me into my mother's shoes so that I can understand why she reacted that way."

Again, I quietly reflected on the Lord. Within a very short time He revealed to me her side of the story. My mother would often be sick for two weeks at a time. She suffered with painful swollen knee joints, as well as urticaria, which is an inflammatory reaction in the skin. We didn't have a housekeeper, so my mother was doing all the housework in her pain. She wasn't angry with me, and she had no intention of not giving me a reward. All she wanted was to get past. The moment the Holy Spirit revealed this to me, I was able to forgive her from the heart. What was amazing was that I heard her saying the same words, "You're in my way!" but now with a mother's gentleness. I had misinterpreted what she was trying to say. So, I said, "Mom, I forgive you and will you please forgive me?" I said those words, even though my mother had died 30 years before.

Now I had to cancel the debts. In my case, I believed that my mother owed me a sweet for the work I had done. I had not received 'payment'; I had judged her by thinking she owed me. In doing so, I had violated the spiritual law of judgment, and this had an effect upon me throughout my working life up to that point. As I reflected on the past, I could see a pattern. I was often not paid what I was worth and occasionally not even paid at all. My whole family had suffered due to my judgment that occurred because of that childhood incident.

Having cancelled the debt regarding this seemingly trivial incident. My life and the lives of those around me began to change for the better. I now have a whole new way of thinking and therefore I am now able to react differently. This is what repentance is all about.

There is a bonus. Before, I had often not been acknowledged for my efforts and commitment but now I am openly recognised for my work and effort.

Appendix 2

SAMPLE PRAYERS

Receiving Christ – God's Plan of Redemption:

Dear God, I have just learnt that I can be part of your Plan of Redemption. Right now, I *(your name)* freely choose your Plan of Redemption, without any coercion.

I *(your name)* have come to realise that no effort or any good deeds of my own, can remove the wrong thoughts and actions from my past or my future. I also realise that if I do not accept your Son, Jesus Christ of Nazareth, that my eternal future is in jeopardy.

So right now, I *(your name)* accept that Jesus Christ of Nazareth, who came to earth, lived exactly as I have lived, has suffered torment as I have suffered torment, and still did not sin. I believe and accept that Jesus Christ of Nazareth, has paid the full price for all I have done wrong and as I now receive Your Plan of Redemption. I am forgiven from all my mess ups, past, present, and future. I now receive Jesus Christ of Nazareth as my Lord and Saviour and as a result, I am a citizen of Heaven and accepted as your child.

Now Father God, I realised my thinking is pretty messed up, so I need some help. Will You please fill me with your Holy Spirit to that I can be changed in a way that is helpful to me and also blesses You.

Thank you, Father God, for it says in the Bible,

"that if you confess with your mouth, "Jesus is Lord," and believe in your heart that God raised Him from the dead, you will be saved."

— ROMANS 10 VERSE 9 —

Amen.

Name: _____ Date: _____

APPENDIX 2

Confession

Heavenly Father, I come to you in the name of Jesus Christ of Nazareth.

Lord these attitudes and emotions of *(name every attitude and emotions experienced)* are not the fruit of the Holy Spirit. I confess them as sin. Lord, please forgive me for allowing bondage and control that is not from you, to come into my life, whether it be consciously or unconsciously, knowingly, or unknowingly.

Lord, these negative emotions are not something that I carry in my hands. They are deep within me, part of my flesh and bones. I have tried to get rid of them, ignore them, control them, and suppress them, but I've always failed. Lord, these feelings overwhelm me and I'm helpless and hopeless before them.

I believe in you, and I believe that you have the power to set me free. I ask you to remove from me all these wrong emotions, feelings, and resultant behaviour. I am unable to help you with the process and if you do not come and set me free, I am going to be stuck with them. I am dependant upon you and despair of any plans or means of my own, or outside assistance and resort only to the hope I have in you. If there be any method that can promise me an escape from these difficulties, I look to you for it.

I thank you for being my deliverer and for setting me free, for it is written:

If I acknowledge and own up to my wrongdoing and offenses, you Heavenly Father are trustworthy, sure, true, and holy to lay aside all my wrongdoing and offenses, and purge and purify me from all moral wrongfulness of character, life, and action.

— 1 JOHN 1:9 —

Amen.

Forgiveness towards others

Heavenly Father, I come to you in the name of Jesus Christ of Nazareth.

Heavenly Father, thank you for your Holy Spirit who has revealed to me why *(name behaved …… and said ……)*. Father in the name of Jesus I forgive and release *(name)* from my heart.

I want to honour *(name)* and thank you for him/her/them. Heavenly Father if he/she/they had known you in your truth and love he/she/they would not have said those things nor behaved that way towards me. If he/she/they really knew how his/her/their words and actions would affect me he/she/they would not have said those things nor behaved that way. I want to say as Jesus said, "Father forgive him/her/them for he/she/they did not know what he/she/they was/were doing" Now I am releasing him/her/them and setting him/her/them free in the name of Jesus and as a result I am now free to be who you created me to be.

Thank you, Heavenly Father, for it is written:

You have given me the keys to the realm of heavenly happiness and power. You declared that whatever I have bound on earth is bound in heaven and whatever I have loosed here on earth is loosened and released in heaven.

— *Matthew 16:19; 18:18* —

Amen.

APPENDIX 2

Forgiving yourself

Seat yourself in the spirit realm in your spirit person and then speak the following prayer over your soul and body in the earthly realm, using your own name.

Heavenly Father, I want to thank you for *(name)*, that you created him/her perfectly in your image. Heavenly Father, through your Holy Spirit, you have revealed to me that *(name)* has grown up in circumstances that have formed his/her negative and wrong way of thinking. That it was and is impossible for *(name)* to behave any differently or speak differently in those circumstances.

Father in the name of Jesus I now forgive and release *(name)* from my heart.

I want to honour *(name)* and thank you for him/her. Heavenly Father if he/she had known you in your truth and love, at that time, he/she would not have said those things nor behaved that way. If he/she really knew how his/her words and actions would affect my life, he/she would not have said those things nor behaved that way. I want to say as Jesus said, "Father forgive *(name)* for he/she did not know what or how to do it differently at that time" Now I am releasing *(name)* and setting him/her free in the name of Jesus and as a result I am now free to be who you created me to be.

Thank you, Heavenly Father, for it is written:

> *You have given me the keys to the realm of heavenly happiness and power. You declared that whatever I have bound on earth is bound in heaven and whatever I have loosed here on earth is loosened and released in heaven.*
>
> — MATTHEW 16:19; 18:18 —

Canceling the debt

Heavenly Father, I come to you in the name of Jesus Christ of Nazareth.

Forgive me for my judgment against *(name)* and any other person who has not met my expectation when it came to *(state incident, receiving what I expected)*. Now Heavenly Father, if I find that somebody does not treat me correctly, from now on it doesn't matter. I can only say this because you, Heavenly Father, have promised me, by your New Covenant with Jesus of which I am a partaker, to provide all my needs[274], to take care of me and to protect me[275]. I now commit my life and my decisions to you, and you have promised to guide me[276].

I now release, cancel, annul any debt that I feel is owed me. I cancel every word, thought or deed and judgment on my part against anybody or person or thing regarding this that I feel is owed me. I set myself free from its influence over my family and me. Thank you, Jesus!

Thank you, Heavenly Father, for it is written:

> *You are able to cause things to happen immediately, beyond and abundantly above all I ask for, desire, am able to comprehend or perceive, and you do it by means of the miraculous and powerful Holy Spirit within me.*
>
> — *(Ephesians 3:20)* —

Amen.

---

[274] Philippians 4:19
[275] Isaiah 43:2
[276] Luke 1:78-79

APPENDIX 2

Repentance:

Heavenly Father, in the name of Jesus Christ of Nazareth, I come to you and confess that I have wrong attitudes and a wrong way of thinking about *(issue)*. Please forgive me from my wrong attitudes and wrong way of thinking. I ask that you, by your Holy Spirit in me, would open the eyes of my heart to see things from your perspective[277]. Give me your revelation about *(issue)* so that by a new understanding my attitudes and thinking are changed.

Lord, I thank you for purifying my heart.

Amen.

---

[277] Matthew 13:15-16

Ancestral iniquity

Under the authority of the New Covenant, I proclaim the blood of Jesus over my family, my possessions, my house and myself for protection. I proclaim that Jesus Christ is Lord and Lord over me.

In the authority of Jesus Christ, I bind all evil spirits and demons in this place and command them not to interfere, make anyone feel uncomfortable or embarrass anyone in any manner or form. I bind and forbid any evil spirit or demon outside this place to interfere or influence what is taking place here.

In the name of Jesus Christ of Nazareth, I bind and rebuke all anti-prayer demons, anti-progress demons, anti-prosperity demons, anti-miracle demons and anti- deliverance demons. I ask the Holy Spirit to destroy every covering Satan has set up against me and around me in the earth, on the earth and in the heavens above. I destroy the web of Satan that he has used to entangle me and loose myself from the powers of darkness.

I ask you Heavenly Father to surround this place with your warrior angels and to fill this place with your ministering angels.

Heavenly Father, I come before your Throne of Grace, in the name of Jesus. Father I bring the sins, transgressions, and iniquities of my ancestors to the tenth generation before you and on their behalf confess their sins of *(practice or act)* as wrong. On their behalf I ask for your forgiveness and that you would cancel, break, sever and destroy the effect of their sins, transgressions and iniquity upon me, and my future generations.

In the name of Jesus, I cancel, break, sever and destroy all curses, utterances, covenants, oaths, and initiations spoken by my ancestors against themselves, against their future generations, and against me. I withdraw my membership from all ungodly initiations or covenants. I cancel my name from Satan's register. I set myself free from all curses, utterances, and oaths.

APPENDIX 2

In the powerful name of Jesus and by the fire of the Holy Spirit, I destroy any place where my name, my image, my pictures, my properties, my clothes, my money, my fingernails, my hair or any parts of my body or any properties of mine are held by demonic forces in the spirit realm. I ask the Holy Spirit to destroy all the items of Satan that are working and testifying against me through the ungodly activities of my ancestors.

I destroy any cage, chain, bag or prison room where Satan has kept my heart imprisoned because of the ungodly activities of my ancestors.

In the name of Jesus, I take back all my rights to my body, to my soul and to my spirit. I reclaim all the parts of myself in the earth, on the earth and in the heavens that were held captive by the ungodly activities of my ancestors. I release from myself any parts of them in me.

Heavenly Father I apply the blood of Jesus to the pathways and to those parts of myself used by demonic spirits to gain access to me through my previous generations. Those pathways and connections are now destroyed, and Satan is now unable to use those connections to rob, kill or destroy from me.

I declare myself free from all iniquities and curses. Heavenly Father rebuke the devourer from my life and according to your Word reverse all curses and oaths and change them into blessings.[278] Give me the former and latter rain[279] and fill me to overflowing with your Holy Spirit. According to your Word, you said that streams of living water would flow from my innermost being.[280] I ask that those streams begin to flow in abundance.

Thank you, Jesus, that you became a curse so that I can be blessed.[281]

Amen.

---

[278] Nehemiah 13:2
[279] Joel 2:23
[280] John 7:38
[281] Galatians 3:13

Intercession on behalf of my previous generations

Heavenly Father, I come to your Throne of Grace, in the name of Jesus Christ of Nazareth.

I stand here on behalf of my family, parents, grandparents on both sides, and my ancestors.

Heavenly Father, thank you for your Holy Spirit who has revealed to me why family, parents, grandparents, ancestors on both sides of my family have failed to keep your commands nor listened to your Word.

On their behalf I confess their sins, transgressions, and iniquities of …

Father in the name of Jesus I ask that you forgive and release *(name)* because of your Word that declares that if we confess their sins and the sins of our ancestors, you will remember your covenants (Leviticus 26 verses 40, 42).

I want to honour *(name)* and thank you for him/her/them. If he/she/they had known how their words and actions would affect my life and the lives of your people, he/she/they would not have said those things nor behaved that way. I want to ask you, Heavenly Father to forgive him/her/them for he/she/they did not know what they were doing.

I make this appeal based on Your purposes for my life and the plans for Your people, to fulfill what You have ordained from the beginning of time. Father, fulfill Your purposes so that those who do not know You can see that You are a righteous God and see that You are good. For I know that You keep your covenant and are faithful and attentive to those called by Your name.

Thank you, Heavenly Father.

APPENDIX 2

Curses

Heavenly Father, I come before your Throne of Grace, in the name of Jesus. Father I have confessed to you my sin, I have forgiven everyone and cancelled all debts that you have revealed to me by your Holy Spirit or that I am consciously aware of.

Under the authority of the New Covenant, I proclaim the blood of Jesus over my family, my possessions, my house and over me for protection. I proclaim that Jesus Christ is Lord and Lord over me. In the authority of Jesus Christ, I bind all evil spirits and demons in this place and command them not to interfere, to make anyone feel uncomfortable or embarrass them in any manner or form. I bind and forbid any evil spirit or demon outside this place to interfere or influence what is taking place here. I ask you Heavenly Father to surround this place with your warrior angels and to fill this place with your ministering angels.

Heavenly Father, I recognize now that I have been struggling with curses and rejection resulting from negative words that were spoken against me by myself and others. By faith, I step from rejection into acceptance in You. Heavenly Father, I commit myself to You and I place my life, my job, my calling, and my future in Your hands. I belong to You.

In the authority of Jesus Christ and through His sacrifice for me on the cross, I break off and nullify any negative words and curses that have been spoken over me by myself or others. I cancel the effect of the following words *(repeat the negative words)* over my life, my family, and my future generations. I renounce those curses and set myself free of the effects of those curses by the power of the blood of Jesus Christ.

In the name of Jesus, I take back all rights to my body, to my soul and to my spirit. Heavenly Father I apply the blood of Jesus to that part of myself where these words resided so that Satan will be unable to use these connections to rob, kill or destroy from me ever again.

A ROAD TO FREEDOM

Thank you, Heavenly Father, that I am set free from all curses and utterances that I have confessed to you today. I declare this in the power and authority of the Lord Jesus Christ. Amen.

APPENDIX 2

Soul ties

Heavenly Father, I come before your Throne of Grace, in the name of Jesus. Father I have confessed to you my sin, I have forgiven everyone and cancelled all debts that you have revealed to me by your Holy Spirit or that I am consciously aware of.

Under the authority of the New Covenant, I proclaim the blood of Jesus over my family, my possessions, my house and over me for protection. I proclaim that Jesus Christ is Lord and Lord over me. In the authority of Jesus Christ, I bind all evil spirits and demons in this place and command them not to interfere, to make anyone feel uncomfortable or embarrass them in any manner or form. I bind and forbid any evil spirit or demon outside this place to interfere or influence what is taking place here. I ask you Heavenly Father to surround this place with your warrior angels and to fill this place with your ministering angels.

Heavenly Father I ask that you please forgive me for allowing bondage and control that is not from you, to come into my life, whether it be consciously or unconsciously, knowingly, or unknowingly. I renounce, break, sever and destroy every ungodly soul tie and bondage created between me and *(names)*. I renounce, break, sever and destroy every ungodly soul tie and bondage that stops me from exercising self-control, renewing my mind or that was formed for the purpose of control, manipulation or domination.

In the name of Jesus, I take back all rights to my body, to my soul and to my spirit. I reclaim all the parts of myself that were connected to *(names)*, and I release from myself any parts of them in me. Heavenly Father I apply the blood of Jesus to that part of myself where these connections existed so that Satan will be unable to use these connections to rob, kill or destroy[282] from me ever again.

---

[282] John 10:10

Thank you, Heavenly Father, that I am set free from all soul ties and connections that I have confessed to you today. I declare this in the power and authority of the Lord Jesus Christ.

Amen.

APPENDIX 2

Spiritual strongholds

(When involved with occult or esoteric practices)

Heavenly Father, I come before your Throne of Grace, in the name of Jesus Christ. Holy Father, I have confessed to you my sin, I have forgiven everyone and cancelled all debts that you have revealed to me by your Holy Spirit or that I am consciously aware of.

Under the authority of the New Covenant, I proclaim the blood of Jesus over my family, my possessions, my house and over myself for protection. I proclaim that Jesus Christ is Lord and Lord over me.

In the authority of Jesus Christ, I bind all evil spirits and demons in this place and command them not to interfere, make anyone feel uncomfortable or embarrass anyone in any manner or form. I bind and forbid any evil spirit or demon outside this place to interfere or influence what is taking place here. In the name of Jesus Christ of Nazareth, I bind and rebuke all anti-prayer demons, anti-progress demons, anti-prosperity demons, anti-miracle demons and anti-deliverance demons. I ask the Holy Spirit to destroy every covering Satan has set up against me and around me in the earth, on the earth and in the heavens above. I destroy the web of Satan that has been used to entangle me and I loose myself from the powers of darkness.

I ask you Heavenly Father to surround this place with your warrior angels and to fill this place with your ministering angels.

In the name of Jesus Christ of Nazareth, now I address you Satan, all evil spirits, servants of Satan, every demon, every demonic power and authority, no matter your level, your rank or area of operation. I declare that I have confessed my sin and my involvement in *(name)* and with all evil practices that are connected to it before the Lord Jesus Christ. It is written that I am forgiven and cleansed from all unrighteousness. Satan and all your demonic hoards now have no rights in my life and you will obey the Word of the Lord as I address you.

A ROAD TO FREEDOM

Spirit of *(name the type of spirit)* I command you in the name of Jesus Christ of Nazareth to leave me now and go to the dry place that has been assigned to you. I command you not to return and try to torment me again.

(Repeat the above for each type of spirit: fear, lies, heaviness, bondage, infirmity, whoredoms, jealousy, haughtiness, antichrist, the deaf and dumb spirit, the perverse spirit, and the familiar spirit. It is sufficient that only the relevant type of spirit need be addressed.)

In the name of Jesus, I cancel, break, sever and destroy all curses, utterances, covenants, oaths, and initiations spoken by me or over me. I withdraw my membership from all ungodly initiations or covenants. I cancel my name from Satan's register. I set myself free from all curses, utterances, and oaths.

In the name of Jesus, I take back all rights to my body, to my soul and to my spirit and reclaim all the parts of myself that were held captive in the earth, on the earth and in the heavens above.

Heavenly Father I apply the blood of Jesus to the pathways and to those parts of myself used by those spirits to gain access. Those pathways and connections are now destroyed, and Satan is now unable to use those connections to rob, kill or destroy[283] from me.

Holy Spirit, I now invite you to come and fill every space left by those demonic spirits in my soul. Fill me to overflowing with love, joy, peace, patience, kindness, goodness, gentleness, faithfulness, and perseverance. According to your Word, you said that streams of living water would flow from my innermost being.[284] I ask that those streams begin to flow in abundance. Jesus, thank you for setting me free. Lord, I give you all the glory.

Amen.

---

[283] John 10:10
[284] John 7:38

APPENDIX 2

Spiritual strongholds

(When **not** involved with occult or esoteric practices)

Heavenly Father, I come before your Throne of Grace, in the name of Jesus Christ. Holy Father, I have confessed to you my sin, I have forgiven everyone and cancelled all debts that you have revealed to me by your Holy Spirit or that I am consciously aware of.

Under the authority of the New Covenant, I proclaim the blood of Jesus over my family, my possessions, my house and over myself for protection. I proclaim that Jesus Christ is Lord and Lord over me.

In the authority of Jesus Christ, I bind all evil spirits and demons in this place and command them not to interfere, make anyone feel uncomfortable or embarrass anyone in any manner or form. I bind and forbid any evil spirit or demon outside this place to interfere or influence what is taking place here. In the name of Jesus Christ of Nazareth, I bind and rebuke all anti-prayer demons, anti-progress demons, anti-prosperity demons, anti-miracle demons and anti-deliverance demons. I ask the Holy Spirit to destroy every covering Satan has set up against me and around me in the earth, on the earth and in the heavens above. I destroy the web of Satan that has been used to entangle me and I loose myself from the powers of darkness.

I ask you Heavenly Father to surround this place with your warrior angels and to fill this place with your ministering angels.

In the name of Jesus Christ of Nazareth, now I address you Satan, all evil spirits, servants of Satan, every demon, every demonic power and authority, no matter your level, your rank or area of operation. I declare that I have confessed my sin before the Lord Jesus Christ. It is written that I am forgiven and cleansed from all unrighteousness. Satan and all your demonic hoards, you have no right in my life and you will obey the Word of the Lord as I address you.

Spirit of *(name the type of spirit)* I command you in the name of Jesus

A ROAD TO FREEDOM

Christ of Nazareth to leave me now and go to the dry place that has been assigned to you. I command you not to return and try to torment me again.

(Repeat the above for each type of spirit: fear, lies, heaviness, bondage, infirmity, whoredoms, jealousy, haughtiness, antichrist, the deaf and dumb spirit, the perverse spirit and the familiar spirit. It is sufficient that only the relevant type of spirit need be addressed.)

In the name of Jesus, I cancel, break, sever and destroy all curses, utterances and oaths spoken by me. I cancel my name from Satan's register and set myself free from the effect of all curses, utterances, and oaths.

In the name of Jesus, I take back all rights to my body, to my soul and to my spirit and reclaim all the parts of myself that were held captive in the earth, on the earth and in the heavens above. Father, I ask you to turn every curse into a blessing.[285]

Heavenly Father I apply the blood of Jesus to the pathways and to those parts of myself used by those spirits to gain access. Those pathways and connections are now destroyed, and Satan is now unable to use those connections to rob, kill or destroy from me.

Holy Spirit, I now invite you to come and fill every space left by those demonic spirits in my soul. Fill me to overflowing with love, joy, peace, patience, kindness, goodness, gentleness, faithfulness, and perseverance. According to your Word, you said that streams of living water would flow from my innermost being[286]. I ask that those streams begin to flow in abundance.

Jesus, thank you for setting me free. Lord, I give you all the glory.

Amen.

---

[285] Nehemiah 13:2
[286] John 7:38

APPENDIX 2

Healing for the wounded spirit

It is the intention that this is prayed over a person with a damaged spirit by the laying on of hands. It is suggested that you hold your hand about 2 centimetres (1 inch) away from the top of the shoulder or crown of the head while the recipient is relaxed and in a comfortable position. Please check with the person before you pray that they are comfortable with your hand over their head.

Heavenly Father, you come before your Throne of Grace, in the name of Jesus. I invite your Holy Spirit to minister to *(name)*. I ask you Holy Spirit to come and restore this broken spirit. Where this spirit has been wounded, bruised, and damaged, please pour in Your oil and the wine to bring healing. Where *(name)* spirit has been trapped, chained, or imprisoned, you ask you to set *(name)* free and draw out their spirit into your marvellous healing light. Where *(name)* spirit has been broken into pieces, you ask that you Holy Spirit will mend, heal and restore *(name)* spirit to become fully functional again.

Holy Spirit, please fill *(name)* up to the very top with love, joy, peace, patience, kindness, goodness, gentleness, faithfulness, and perseverance. According to your Word, You said that streams of living water would flow from their innermost being.[287] I now ask that those streams begin to flow in abundance. Lord, we give you all the glory in Christ Jesus.

Amen.

(It is suggested that you now remain silent, while still laying on of hands and let the Holy Spirit minister. You should not be hasty or interfere with what the Holy Spirit may be doing. Continue praying silently until the person being prayed for chooses to engage with you.)

---

[287] John 7:38

Difficult situations

Holy Father, Father of Abraham, Isaac, and Jacob, you are completely aware that it is beyond my human strength and ability to avoid the present situation and difficulties I now find myself in. I choose to look only to you and to your hand of deliverance, to get me out of these difficulties. I despair of any plans or means of my own, or outside assistance and resort only to the hope I have in you. If there be any method that can promise me an escape from *(issue)*, I look to you for it.

Father manifest your power and let it come quickly and raise me up to be of good courage and faith to believe in you for deliverance.

I am in a helpless place, but still it is a place that you possess; the sea is yours, the valleys and the mountains that surround me are yours and if you would simply speak your Word, the mountains would become level plains and the sea would open up and become dry land.

Yes Father, at your command every situation will change, every difficulty will fade, and every need will be provided for, and every curse will become a blessing, for it is your will to prosper me, provide for me, to protect me and deliver me.

Thank you, Father, in Jesus' name.

Amen.

Appendix 3

UNPLEASANT FEELING WORDS

Abandoned	Dubious	Longing	Scared
Adamant	Dumbfounded	Low	Screwed-up
Aggravated		Lustful	Sensitive
Agony	Empty		Shocked
Ambivalent	Envious	Mad	Silly
Angry	Evil	Maudlin	Sly
Annoyed	Exasperated	Mean	Sneaky
Anxious	Exhausted	Melancholy	Sorrowful
Apathetic		Miserable	Spiteful
Assertive	Fearful		Squeezed
Astounded	Flustered	Naughty	Startled
	Foolish	Nervous	Stingy
Bad	Frantic	Niggardly	Strange
Betrayed	Feeble		Stunned
Bitter	Frightened	Obnoxious	Stupefied
Burdened	Frustrated	Obsessed	Stupid
	Furious	Opposed	Suffering
Cheated		Oppressed	
Childish	Greedy	Outraged	Tempted
Competitive	Grief	Overwhelmed	Tense
Condemned	Guilty		Tentative
Confused		Painful	Tenuous
Conspicuous	Hateful	Panicked	Terrible
Contrite	Helpless	Persecuted	Terrified
Cruel	Horrible	Petrified	Threatened

Crushed	Hurt	Pitiful	Thwarted
Culpable	Hysterical	Precarious	Tired
		Pressured	Trapped
Deceitful	Ignored	Pulled-apart	Troubled
Defeated	Immoral		
Dependant	Immortal	Quarrelsome	Ugly
Despair	Infuriated	Queer	Uneasy
Destructive	Intimidated		Unsettled
Diminished	Isolated	Rage	
Discontented		Rejected	Violent
Disdain	Jealousy	Remorse	Vulnerable
Distracted	Jumpy	Restless	
Distraught		Rushed	Weepy
Disturbed	Lecherous	Regret	Wicked
Divided	Licentious		Worried
Dominated	Lonely	Sad	

Please note: this is not an exhaustive list.

Appendix 4

ABRIDGED LIST OF SPIRITUAL STRONGHOLDS

Spirit of Bondage

Romans 8:15 talks about a spirit of slavery, oppression, or bondage. This may be characterised by feelings of anguish, bitterness, brokenness, and lustfulness. The person may experience feelings of being blinded, bruised, broken, oppressed, and held captive while outward manifestations may be addictions, greediness, an excessive desire for gain, ambition, and compulsive desires.

Spirit of Heaviness

Isaiah 61:3 mentions a spirit of heaviness with undertones of weakness and darkness. This may be characterised by feelings of being feeble, obscure, sorrowful, sad, troubled, despair, hopelessness, gloominess, rejection, and self-pity. People oppressed by this spirit often feel discouraged, isolated and in continual mourning.

Spirit of Lies

1 Kings 22:22-23 and 2 Chronicles 18:21-22 refer to a lying, untruthful, deceitful, or false spirit. People tormented by this spirit may be deluded and have vain imaginations or notions. They often struggle with a driving

zeal or frenzied emotions sometimes acted out in religious activities. They tend to insinuate or exaggerate while using flattery or alternatively profanity. Hypocrisy and superstitions also characterise this type of spirit.

Spirit of Fear

2 Timothy 1:7 refers to a spirit of fear or timidity.

People struggling with these types of spirit are fearful, frightened, tormented, terrified, tense, agitated, full of horror, dread, apprehension, and anxiety. They may experience trembling, shyness, and worry a lot. They often struggle with nightmares, a fear of dying, phobias, and heart attacks, feelings of inadequacy and inferiority.

Spirit of Infirmity

Luke 13:11 discusses a woman with a spirit of infirmity. This may include feebleness, disease or sickness of both body and mind. Such people may continually struggle with colds, fevers, viruses, infections, fungal infections, sinusitis, or hay fever. They may be frail or hunchback in stature or suffer with asthma or arthritis.

Spirit of Whoredoms

Whoredoms, prostitution, lewdness and harlotry are some of the words used in different translations of Hosea 4:12 and Hosea 5:4. Although there is a strong sexual implication, idolatry in any form that replaces God is included in the spirit of whoredoms. Besides those involved in the sex traffic trade, people with this spirit may lust after position, status, money, food, physical gratification, and a hedonistic lifestyle.

Spirit of Jealousy

Numbers 5:14 and 5:30 refer to the spirit of jealousy or envy. This spirit often drives people into competitiveness or causes people to try to be like others. People with this spirit may struggle with anger, rage, spitefulness, or cruelty. They may covet, be suspicious, selfish, murderous or seek revenge when wronged. Another characteristic is that it tries to separate friends, families, and church communities.

Deaf and dumb spirit

In Mark 9:25 it is recorded that Jesus cast a deaf and dumb spirit out of a man. It refers to the senses of speech and hearing being impaired. This spirit may cause convulsions, schizophrenia, seizures, epilepsy, ear and eye diseases, and dumbness. Outward signs may be foaming at the mouth, suffering, gnashing of the teeth, crying, suicidal tendencies and hydrophobia, while it may also compel and drive one towards insanity.

Perverse spirit

The perverse spirit causes a person to be crooked, wicked, to do the wrong thing or be contrary. It may be characterised by being perverse, rebellious, and foolish. People under its influence may despise, hate, lust, fret, be lovers of self, false teachers and prone to error. They are often ensnared by false ideas and go astray as referred to in Isaiah 19:14.

Spirit of Pride

A spirit of haughtiness or pride is referred to in Proverbs 16:18. It is recognised by feelings and expressions of arrogance, conceit, self-importance, over confidence, superiority, self-righteousness, and grandeur. Other manifestations are scorning, mockery, bragging, stubbornness, obstinacy, egotistical behaviour, contentiousness, and vanity. People inflicted with this spirit may be dictatorial, arrogant, insolent, stiff-necked, and have an air of superiority. They are also prone to gossip. This spirit may also take on a form of self-demeaning, false martyrdom and self-denial often letting everyone know how much he or she had to give up.

Spirit of Antichrist

Reference is made to this spirit in 1 John 4:3. This spirit opposes Christ by trying to substitute everything of God, which will include signs and powerful acts. It will often openly attack people, their testimonies, ministries, and the gifts of the Spirit at the same time as persecuting them. It likes to set itself up as an authority, making bold claims, uttering blasphemies, while it tries to intimidate, suppress, irritate, and seduce into error.

Familiar Spirit

This type of spirit is discussed in Leviticus 20:27, Deuteronomy 18:11, 1 Samuel 28:7-8, 1 Chronicles 10:13, 2 Chronicles 33:6, Isaiah 19:3, and Isaiah 29:4. This spirit refers to the consultation with any person to gain knowledge or enlightenment that is occultic or esoteric in nature. This includes the consultation of idols, mediums, charmers, white witches, wizards, hypnotists, fortune tellers, astrologers and divining in any form.

Printed in Great Britain
by Amazon